A Year in My Garden

Nancy Chaplin

First published in 2002 by
Professional Marketing International
Warnford Court
29 Throgmorton Street
London
EC2N 2AT

Printed in England

ISBN 0-9542922-0-0

"For my mother who inspired me and so many others with a love of gardening"

Nancy and her husband in the courtyard garden of The Yard House in September 1982

Arthur and Nancy Chaplin converted the stableyard of Little Berkhamsted
House and moved there in February 1976

◁ PREFACE ▷

EVERY garden changes and develops each year. This book covers many years in my garden. It is derived from monthly articles that I wrote between 1982 and 2000 whilst Gardening Correspondent of the *Hartford Hundred* parish magazine.

We have had dry summers when I lost plants, and cold winters when tender shrubs did not survive. Some of my original plantings grew too large, and had to be hard-pruned or thrown out. Others have been eaten by muntjak deer. This is the great interest of gardening: each year is different and presents new challenges.

The photographs were taken when that part of the garden was at its best, so in many ways they make everything look almost too perfect – but this is true of all garden photographs.

I am grateful to my brother, Simon Bond, who has given me so much help and good advice, as well as plants from his small specialist Nursery Garden; to all my many gardening friends who have been so generous with plants and cuttings from their gardens; and to all those who open their gardens to the public. Other people's gardens are always such a source of inspiration. Above all, I thank Lord and Lady Salisbury, in whose wonderful gardens at Hatfield House I learnt so much during the twenty years that I was privileged to work as a Garden Guide.

Finally, I am grateful to my family, particularly my son Richard and daughter-in-law Norma who both encouraged me to publish this book, and helped with plant names and design, and to Sue Jacobs for typing the manuscript.

Nancy Chaplin
May 2002

The woodland garden in May. Pink saxifrage oppositifolia (mossy
saxifrage) in foreground. Euphorbia robbiae under the beech trees.

❧ CONTENTS ❧

⚡ LOOKING AT THE GARDEN
IN WINTER ⚡

JANUARY seems to me a good month to take stock in the garden and look out at it from the windows for ideas in planting which might improve that look in the future. Perhaps it would pay to be strong-minded and get rid of some shrub, which has outgrown its position or become straggly with old age, then you will have the fun of deciding what to replace it with. It may take a year or two for that part of the garden to look balanced again, but in gardening you must be prepared to take a long term view.

Some small shrubs such as **perennial wallflowers**, or *Erysimum* (syn. *Cheiranthus*), are really better replaced at regular intervals. They root so easily and grow so quickly that cuttings, taken in early summer, will be ready to put out in the autumn and will flower well next spring. I only grow one *Erysimum*, the rather inaptly named **'Bowles' Mauve'**, which is not mauve at all, but a lovely rich purple. It makes a neat evergreen bush and gives you a wonderful splash of colour in May after which, if you keep it well dead-headed, will continue to flower all summer. But after two or three years it will begin to straggle and look leggy, and then I throw it out and start again.

Most grey-leafed shrubs can be kept neat by a drastic pruning in April when any danger of frost is over. But they can die back in old age, or just get too big however much you cut them back, and then it is surely better to root cuttings and start again. *Senecio greyi*, the New Zealand bush, behaves rather differently, as the flower stems die right back after flowering, so it is better to cut them back in August and they will break and form a neat bush again before the winter. As they are quite hardy, their silver-grey leaves contribute a lot to the winter garden.

1

Never forget that to cut anything back encourages new soft growth and that the majority of shrubs are better pruned immediately after flowering. It is very unwise to prune evergreens, or ever-greys, in the late autumn or winter months – wait until the spring.

Take another moment to look out of your favourite windows – perhaps where you sit during meals or from behind your kitchen sink – and think about your garden. Do you like what you see in the bleak landscape? Have you given your garden enough interesting shapes to please the eye when there are no flowers to enjoy? Some evergreens strategically placed are really essential for this, and perhaps some golden foliage to catch the low winter sunshine – or colourful twigs such as the red-stemmed *Cornus*.

When thinking of evergreens, the first choice might be **conifers**, of which such a great variety in all shapes and colours are now available in every garden centre. Care must be taken not to plant those which seem perfect when young, but which can very easily outgrow their allotted space. For this reason they are not easy to place, particularly as they dislike being crowded by other plants. Some of us are fortunate enough to have an acid soil, and thus are able to plant *Rhododendrons* but they too take up a lot of space. An alternative might be *Viburnum tinus* or *Laurustinus*, which makes a large and shapely bush with the added advantage of winter flowers. In a shady corner, the *Skimmias* grow happily, although you need a male and a female form to enjoy their colourful red berries. The shrubby *Euonymus*, with lovely variegated leaves is always a safe choice, and two other delightful small evergreens are *Osmanthus delavayi*, which has tiny holly-like leaves and intensely sweet smelling flowers in May, and the humble little *Sarcococcas*, members of the **box** (*buxus*) family. The latter will flourish in dense shade, but deserve to be planted near a path where you can enjoy their tiny but heavily scented white flowers in mid-winter.

Another large family of evergreens which make neat round bushes is the New Zealand **Hebes**. I find the small-leafed varieties completely hardy, but those with larger leaves and longer flower tassels will not survive a harsh winter.

There are quite a number of different *Cornuses*, or dogwoods, as they are called in North America where most of them originate; and most will develop into small trees or sucker and form a dense thicket of low growing twigs if left to their own devices. These suckers are not for the small garden; they will rapidly outgrow their welcome. The common red-stemmed dogwood, even in its more desirable variegated form is very invasive, but *C.* **alba 'Sibirica'**, sometimes known as the Westonbirt variety, is a wonderful plant. It should be severely pruned each spring to ensure the fresh growth of young wood to colour ruby-red the following winter.

✃ HERBS FOR THE POT ✄

AS soon as they have recovered from Christmas keen gardeners are supposed to start studying their seed lists. I really prefer a month or two when I forget about the garden, but I was recently asked to write about herbs, and most of these are easily raised from seed.

These are the ones which I find easy to grow. We can all start with **parsley** (*Petroselinum crispum*), which doesn't always succeed with me. Often it germinates and then the leaves turn yellow and die. I think this is due to attack by carrot fly, and the best thing is to sow a short row fairly often – and hope for the best! Late seedlings are more likely to survive and it is well worthwhile to pot one up for the kitchen window-sill in winter.

Another invaluable herb is **basil** (*Ocimum basilicum*), which needs heat to germinate; it should be sown in the greenhouse in late spring and then treated as a pot plant. I have also tried fresh coriander, but didn't find I used it enough to be worth the effort. **Rosemary** (*Rosmarinus officinalis*), of course, is a shrub, with lovely blue flowers in early spring, and invaluable in a dry, sunny part of the flower garden.

Most of the rest are perennial. **Mint** (*Mentha spicata*) is a nuisance, best planted in a container sunk in the ground, where it cannot escape to run everywhere. **Thyme** (*Thymus vulgaris*) and **marjoram** (*Origanum vulgare*) strike easily from cuttings and like a sunny well-drained position, as do **chives**. The only other two herbs I grow are **French tarragon** (*Artemisia dracunculus*) and **sorrel** (*Rumex scutatus*). Both of these I find invaluable.

Sorrel (*Rumex scutatus*) is lovely in soup with cucumber and potato, and makes a delicious sauce for fish. The flavour is sharp and lemony. I grew this originally from seed, but weeded it out to one plant, which makes a big clump that comes up every year. French tarragon, and it must be French (*A. dracunculus,* as above) – the Russian kind (*A. **dracunculoides***) has much bigger leaves and practically no flavour - is not fully hardy. I bought my plant and keep it in a pot, which goes into the greenhouse when it dies down in autumn. It is an *Artemisia* and dislikes cold and wet. I have tried striking cuttings from it, but without success.

❧ PLANTING TREES AND SHRUBS ❧

THOSE of you who watch that excellent programme called *Gardener's World* may once have seen Geoff Hamilton demonstrating how to plant a tree; explaining that there is no point in digging a hole for it in heavy soil without breaking up

4

and enriching the surrounding area. Without this precaution the hole will act as a sump, into which water drains back, rotting the roots of the young tree.

That made me think about all the rules for successful planting. I have always gardened on the principle that if anything seems to me to be in the wrong place, I shall try to move it somewhere else at the appropriate season. Most plants survive this treatment quite happily.

As a general rule, it is wiser to move evergreens in the autumn, which gives them time to get established before really cold weather, or the drying winds of spring. The moving of deciduous plants should, if possible, be completed before the end of March when they will be stirring into life. Container grown plants from a nursery or garden centre can go in much later, but it is vitally important to water them well before you start; in hot weather dig your planting hole well ahead, and fill it with water which will soak into the ground below the plant. Then install the plant in the evening, so that it has the cool night to settle in. Most gardeners already know this from transplanting annuals, or **lettuces** or **brassicas** in the vegetable garden, which may well have to be done in dry weather. If the roots are in a tight ball in the container, unravel them carefully and spread them out, so that they have a chance to strike out into the surrounding soil.

By sticking to these rules you can successfully move most plants, even in summer (though not when in full flower) and if moving house take some of your treasures with you. Water them well for a few days first, then dig them up and wrap the roots in polythene for the journey – and dig and water the hole before settling them into their new homes.

✣ CHOOSING YOUR CONIFERS ✣

HOW dreary the winter garden would look without a few conifers. There are certainly a great number to choose from. Some stay obligingly dwarf, but there are a great many that look charming and enticing in their containers at a garden centre, but will grow away very fast and eventually become quite large trees taking up a lot of space in the garden. So do check before you buy them.

The largest family of garden conifers, with the greatest variety in size, colour and growth are the false cypresses, *Chamaecyparis*. This is an easy name to remember as it is pronounced SHAMMY-SIP-AR-IS, which you can think of as "sham-cypress". They have feathery foliage and a very attractive growth, and the tall ones clip well and make a good quick-growing hedge. These are *C. lawsoniana*, and *C. l.* **'Green Hedger'** is the one most commonly used. For a tall (up to 30 ft.) but narrow evergreen tree, *C. l.* **'Columnaris'** is probably the best choice, with blue-green foliage. *C. l.* **'Triomf van Boskoop'** has much the same habit, but is a faster grower. There is also another *lawsoniana* with golden foliage called *'Erecta Aurea'*.

These all originate from Oregon. The smaller types of *Chamaecyparis*, however, *C. obtusa* and *C. pisifera* come from Japan. Basically, *obtusas* have compact, fan-shaped whorls of branches. The larger ones will eventually reach five or six feet in height and spread, but there are many dwarf forms suitable for rock gardens. They are dark green, but there are some golden and variegated forms. The *pisiferas* also come in many colours, shapes and sizes and have delicate feathery foliage. *C.p.* **'Boulevard'** is a particularly attractive one, a lovely steely blue. It colours better if grown in part shade, and is very slow growing, forming a shapely conical bush up to four to six feet in height. Another type altogether is *C.p.* **'Filifera'**, which has long weeping cord-like branches. My favourite of all conifers is a vivid golden form of this called *C.p.* **'Filifera Aurea'**. It eventually makes a rounded mound of weeping growth, four to five feet tall, sweeping the ground and covering a circle six to seven feet across and is a magnificent sight if carefully placed, perhaps in the angle or point of a shrub border when it can be seen from three sides.

One final note of caution: if we have snow, do remember to knock it off your conifers before it freezes on and the branches are broken by the weight.

Most of the dwarf ***Picea*** or Spruce make small, shapely bushes with typical pine needle foliage, although there is one attractive prostrate variety. They are all both slow growing and difficult to propagate, so are not easily obtainable, but the silvery-blue varieties are real treasures and well worth looking for. They grow best on light, sandy soil in full sun.

The **juniper** is probably the best known and loved of all garden conifers, both in its narrow upright and prostrate ground-hugging forms. Those thin, dark green columns, which form such effective punctuation marks in amongst heathers or other low growing shrubs are *Juniperus communis 'Hibernica'* or the **Irish Juniper**. They will eventually grow to six to eight feet, though never much more than a foot wide. The real dwarf is *J. communis 'Compressa'* – the **Noah's Ark Juniper**, a compact little column, pale silvery green in colour, growing less than half an inch a year. I have had one in a trough for more than thirty years and it is still only two feet high, though it might perhaps have been a little taller planted in open ground.

The prostrate form is *J. horizontalis*, the **creeping juniper**, which will in time spread out over quite a large area, completely smothering any other growth and never more than eighteen inches high – I have used it quite effectively to cover an old tree stump. The steely blue *J.h. Glauca* is probably the best form.

✣ WINTER FLOWERS AND FOLIAGE ✣

THERE are a few invaluable plants, which help to furnish the
garden by producing their leaves and even flower in mid-winter.
They have corms or bulbous roots and come from countries
where most of the rainfall is in winter or spring, and so the
leaves develop then, to take advantage of the moisture and store
away goodness to see them through the hot, dry summers.

Iris stylosa (now called *Iris unguicularis*) is one. It comes from
Algeria and produces its lovely fragile blooms all through the
winter.

The little autumn flowering *cyclamen* throws up a carpet of
leaves after its delicate flowers have faded, but another hardy
species called *C. coum* waits until January or February to push
up its bright pink curled back petals, even through ice and snow.
I like to plant these where they can be seen from the house
windows and find they seed freely and increase rapidly. They
disappear completely in the summer and are quite happy to be
hidden under the emergent leaves of *hostas* and other
herbaceous plants.

Another very useful winter plant is the **variegated arum**, not
unlike our native **Lords and Ladies**, but with larger and most
beautifully marbled leaves, which appear in late autumn. This
is *Arum italicum* subsp. *italicum 'Marmoratum'* (syn. *A.
pictum*) and comes, I imagine, from the wooded areas in the
south of Italy, as like the *cyclamen*, they are happiest in partial
shade. I grow them at the back of a narrow border against an
east-facing wall in our courtyard. In front of them are the
summer flowering white **arum lilies** (*Zantedeschia aethiopica*),
which die down in winter, moisture loving irises and more
hostas, which die back leaving the green and white arum leaves
in sole possession. They will produce their handsome pale
green flowers in the spring, turning to drumsticks of bright

8

orange berries as the leaves wither and summer progresses, and shedding these berries only as fresh leaves appear the following autumn. I believe they are very poisonous, so perhaps it is a plant to be wary of if young children play in your garden.

⁂ EARLY FLOWERING BULBS – PARTICULARLY SNOWDROPS ⁂

FEBRUARY is the month when the garden wakes into life and is in many ways the most exciting time of the year. Unless the ground is still in the grip of frost, green shoots of early bulbs are poking up everywhere. It should be possible even in the smallest garden to tuck in some clumps of these little early bulbs. It is particularly worthwhile if you can find a place close to the house and enjoy them through the windows or perhaps near a doorway where they will greet you as you go out and welcome you home again. They will be happy to grow underneath the leaves of any plant that dies back in winter, when they can enjoy light and air, and once their foliage has died down they will retreat underground until the following spring.

The first to show flowers are *Leucojum vernum*, the **Spring Snowflake**, opening their white bells tipped with green soon after Christmas. The green shoots of **snowdrops** (*Galanthus*) should be beginning to show at the same time, and will flower this month.

Both *leucojums* and snowdrops seem to prefer moist shady soil, and when happy they increase very rapidly. There is no more breathtaking sight on a fine day early in spring than a carpet of snowdrops, and the best place I know to enjoy them is the garden of The Lordship at Benington, which is open on Sunday afternoons when they are in flower. There they carpet both sides of a grassy moat that circles one side of the garden.

There are, of course, many different varieties of snowdrops, all with slightly different markings. Apart from the **common snowdrop**, (*Galanthus nivalis*), the one that does best with me is a taller and later one called *G. plicatus* **'Warham'**. This comes from the Crimea, and the original bulbs are said to have been sent back to his sister in Ireland by a soldier serving in the Crimean War. Coming from a country sun-baked in summer, they are happier in rather drier conditions than nivalis. All snowdrops hate to be dried out, so it is best to move them immediately the flowers are over and while the leaves are still green. Remember the rules for planting bulbs! They should have twice as much soil over them as their own height, for snowdrops about two inches.

✃ MORE EARLY BULBS ✄

Snowdrops will usually be gone by early March, but the main colour and interest still comes from early-flowering bulbs. *Crocuses* and *scillas* take over, to be followed by the pale blue *chionodoxa*, the even paler stars of *ipheion*, and then the first **daffodils** (*Narcissi*).

The little species *crocuses* come first. Everyone should try to establish a colony of the slender mauve *C. tommasinianus* They need a well-drained soil and plenty of light in spring, and will not grow in grass, but seem quite happy under deciduous trees and seed very quickly and freely. My woodland garden is carpeted with them and when they open on a fine day, the effect is breathtaking. *C. chrysanthus* are sturdier, like a miniature form of the ordinary Dutch crocuses, and they grow in little clumps in predominantly pale yellow and creamy shades.

I have always loved the brilliant gentian blue flowers of **Scilla siberica**. Another pale blue scilla is called *S. tubergeniana*, and the two look lovely together. They do best in a warm sunny position.

The tiny bulbous **irises** are out at the same time and I think they prefer not to be in full sun. *I. histriodes*, the earliest, comes with the snowdrops, and I find them more attractive than the purple *I. reticulata*. They are shorter and sturdier, increase rapidly and are a lovely bright blue.

I now begin to watch for the spotted leaves of **dog-toothed violets**, *Erythronium dens-canis*, which appear almost overnight. Next time you look, they are flowering, surprisingly large deep pink flowers with swept back petals, like a **cyclamen**. These are not bulbs and get their name from their small pointed tubers, like a dog's fangs.

Blue again are the starlike flowers of the *Ipheions*, small members of the onion family. They like full sunshine and are great colonisers. The pale blue white-centred *Chionodoxa* called **Glory of the Snow** (either *C. forbesii* or *C. luciliae*), has the same tastes and resembles the scillas with several flowers on each stalk. They will come out late in March with the early daffodils, which are perhaps the most welcome of all as a sign that the days are really lengthening and that the clocks will soon change.

✄ TASKS FOR SPRING ✄

SPRING is, or should be, much the busiest time in the garden. The work we put in during February, March or April will make all the difference to the amount of time that will have to be spent weeding and tidying up later on in the year.

So if you haven't already done so choose a suitable day, weed your borders carefully, apply a general fertiliser and prick it in carefully with a fork and then apply all the mulch you can make or afford. This will help to conserve moisture in the soil and keep down the weeds and also make it much easier to pull up any that seed in during the summer. I have always used blood, fish and bone as a fertiliser, but this year think of taking the advice of a well-known garden writer and use the rather more expensive Vitax P.4, which is a slow release fertiliser, which should feed the soil all summer.

Do put the mulch on really thickly around newly planted trees or shrubs. Another vital chore is to treat all paths and gravel areas with a weed-killer containing simazine, which inhibits the growth of annual weeds. If your paths are weedy already you will need to use paraquat first, or a combination of weed-killer such as Pathclear. Water it in with a weed-killer bar on a large plastic watering can, which is kept for garden chemicals only, and choose a day when the top layer of gravel is dry but the ground is still damp underneath. You can then see as you go along which area has already been treated. Simazine needs to soak into the top layer of soil to be effective, but doesn't seem to leach sideways like sodium chlorate, though I would never go right up to a grass edge.

For perennial weeds you really need Round-up, now available everywhere, but very difficult to use among plants. It is now also available ready mixed in a "gun" and I think this well worth the money. It squirts out a jet of fine spray, which is easy to control and to direct on to weed growth without wetting surrounding plants. Good quality rubber gloves are essential for all these tasks.

❧ POTTING AND RE-POTTING ❧

MARCH and April are good months to have work to do in the greenhouse, now beginning to be warmed by spring sunshine, and perhaps fragrant with spring flowering pot plants. I have a large *Jasminum polyanthum*, the lovely half-hardy Mediterranean one in mine which fills the air with scent.

Almost everything will benefit from an annual repot. Mix up a barrowful of good quality compost (half general purpose, quarter grit and quarter leaf mould enriched with Osmacote or some other long lasting fertiliser, would be a good mix) perhaps adding some J.R. This would give it more body but a gritty open texture is really important.

Knock the plants out of their pots and shake off old compost (which can be spread anywhere in the garden to improve the soil texture) then re-pot probably in the same pot but using your new mixture, firm down, water well and the plant will grow on gratefully. For very large pots this may be difficult to achieve every year, but at least scrape away as much surface soil as possible and replace with fresh compost.

And of course, now is also the moment to think of starting off half-hardy annuals and vegetable seeds if they are not already in.

❧ PLANTS FOR SHADE ❧

IF your garden is shady, or has shady areas, you may have problems in deciding how to plant it, but ultimately it will look more attractive and be easier to manage than large areas in full sun, which dry out in summer and will need constant deadheading to look their best.

The most difficult shade to cope with is dense evergreen cover
of trees and shrubs, but even with these you may be able to let
in a little light by pruning out the lower branches. The ground
under deciduous trees and shrubs is much less of a problem, as
many of the early bulbs and spring flowers will grow happily
there and disappear underground before the overhead leaves
open and shut out the light. It is important to understand that
shade-lovers are nearly all woodland plants which expect a cosy
carpet of dead leaves to shelter and nourish them every year, so
they will need regular mulching in order to do well.

Some of us do have acid soils where rhododendrons and azaleas
will flourish in the shade, and provide all the colour needed in
spring and early summer, but even on clay soils there are
alternatives. *Mahonia japonica* and *Viburnum tinus* are two
evergreens that tolerate shade and have lovely flowers, and the
majority of the deciduous *viburnums* are woodland plants and
do not enjoy full sun.

On north facing walls the climbing *Hydrangea anomala*
petiolaris is perfectly at home, as are **honeysuckles** (*Lonicera*)
and most *clematis*, provided they can get their heads up into the
sunshine to flower. Try an evergreen climber, *Garrya elliptica*
with long green catkins in early spring, or one of the many
variegated *Euonymus*. The green and white *E. fortunei*
'Emerald Gaiety' is my favourite. Plant a *clematis* at the same
time to give you flowers later, but remember they need rich soil
and a lot of water and the base of a wall is a dry place. At their
feet *hostas*, *rodgersias*, *euphorbias* and *hellebores* have
handsome leaves, as do all the **ferns**. All would look equally well
among shrubs, as do the *hydrangeas*, which will provide colour in
summer and autumn; *Alchemilla* is happy anywhere but does best
in shade. *Brunnera macrophylla* is another shade-lover, with
heart-shaped leaves and Forget-me-not flowers in the spring.

The herbaceous *Geranium endresii* and *G. macrorrhizum* make
good ground cover and a splash of colour. *Tiarella cordifolia*,

the foam flower, is another carpeter with charming leaves and the feathery white flowers which give it its common name.

❧ GARDENING IN LAYERS ❧

I read an article recently extolling the advantages of planning for constant colour and effect in a small garden by what the author called "gardening in layers" and realised that this is very much what I myself am always trying to achieve. In other words, it is the art of getting both pleasure and interest from your plants by planning for succession, and growing one plant through another.

I have often suggested that early spring bulbs can be planted between plants such as *hostas*, which die down in winter. You can carry this idea further with tall summer-flowering bulbs such as **lilies** and *galtonias* between early flowering shrubs such as **azaleas**.

Hardy *fuchsias* and many of the grey-leafed shrubs don't make much growth until the late summer. They are, therefore, very useful to take over from June flowering herbaceous plants, many of which can be cut back after flowering. *Fuchsias*, of course, are cut down to the ground in spring and grey-leafed plants benefit from being trimmed quite toughly after all possibility of damage by frost has passed.

Yet another layer of colour can be provided by the careful use of late flowering *clematis*. Those that flower in May and June cannot be used in this way as they flower on the old wood and should not be severely pruned, but the C. *'Jackmanii'* or C. *viticella* types flower on new growth and should be cut down to within a foot or so from the ground in early spring – and if trained into and over a spring-flowering shrub, will cover it with colour later in the summer.

Never plant a *clematis* too close to its host plant. They are greedy feeders and need plenty of moisture to get well established. A large planting hole should be dug and filled with enriched soil and a support provided to enable the clematis to grow up into the branches of the host shrub. Obviously, one should be careful not to allow the *viticella* types, and certainly not the *C. montanas*, to throttle a delicate shrub, and even the larger *C. 'Jackmanii'* hybrids need a tough host. **Shrub roses** are ideal, also ***Chaenomeles, forsythias*** or ***viburnums***.

⚔ MAGNOLIAS ⚔

I have been told that the *magnolias*, which will soon be opening their exquisite flower cups, are among the survivors of prehistoric plants that flourished before the ice Age, in the days of the dinosaurs. Their flowers are unique in having no sepals. Their petals are slightly fleshy in texture; some are pure white, others flushed with pink or with a purple stain at the base of the petals, and one variety is deep purple.

They are completely hardy and will flourish in almost any soil, tolerating both neglect and any amount of cold weather, although once open the flowers can be browned by frost or cold winds. However, they very much dislike having their roots disturbed and do not move happily. So it is important to give them plenty of space when you plant them. The larger varieties develop into small trees and look best as single specimens in grass.

M. stellata the smallest and probably the easiest one to fit into the average garden. It has pure white flowers, star-shaped rather than cup-shaped. Once settled in, it grows quickly, flowering generously when still quite small.

The late June flowering varieties are rather different in that the flowers open after the leaves and hang downward – lampshades rather than goblets. They are deliciously scented.

All these come from China, but a quite different evergreen *magnolia*, aptly named **grandiflora**, comes from the southern United States, and in England needs the shelter of a south or west wall. It is a most handsome plant with double flowers with a wonderful lemony fragrance. You may have to wait some years and for a hot summer before you can enjoy these, but they are worth waiting for. The *M. g.* **'Exmouth'** variety is considered to be the best for our climate.

✄ PRUNING ROSES ✄

I went to a most interesting talk recently – given by the Secretary of The Rose Society, which he called "Old Wives' Tales in The Garden". He was obviously an experienced and knowledgeable gardener and, of course, a rosarian. He told us about, and showed us slides of trials that had been carried out in the last few years in the Society's Chiswell Green Rose Gardens, which exposed the fallacy of many of our preconceived ideas as to how to look after roses.

For the past six years they had experimented with trial beds, each planted with three blocks of an identical bush rose. One block was pruned in the conventional way by opening out the centre of the bush, removing twiggy growth and pruning the strong growth to an outward facing bud; another block by simply cutting down all the stems to the required height without looking for buds or doing any thinning out; and the third by using a hedge trimmer to achieve the same result. The consistent results were surprising.

In every case, the conventionally pruned roses did less well, carried fewer flowers and were more prone to disease than those treated by the other two methods. On the whole, he suggested that it was better to use secateurs rather than a trimmer, which would scatter the prunings, taking longer to tidy up. His own opinion was that these novel pruning methods led to stronger bushes, because they would carry more leaves on the twiggy growths which would otherwise have been cut out; therefore, they got more nourishment, as plants feed through their leaves as well as from their roots.

Other experiments showed that two early preventative sprays at fortnightly intervals (he recommended Nimrod T) should take care of black spot, and that two sprinklings of rose fertiliser – one in the early spring and the other after the first blooming – should be adequate feeding. A mulch in spring was always beneficial to conserve moisture.

I don't personally find blackspot much of a problem, although I may get a little in the autumn. Some years ago I did read that the important time to spray was at leaf-break in early spring. I am certainly going to save myself a lot of time by cutting back instead of pruning this spring. It will be interesting to see the results. As to when to do so, it makes sense to me to prune and tie in climbers in late autumn, and to prune the rose bushes in February as the buds begin to break. In a very cold winter this might not be until March. I do cut back and shorten a bit in autumn to remove the last dead head.

Our speaker also thought that roses are perfectly happy to be underplanted with other plants, which greatly improve the look of a rose bed. Here again, I entirely agree, and have been doing this for some years.

❧ EUPHORBIAS ❧

THE many different forms of *Euphorbia,* or Spurge as we call
our native wild form, are among the most exciting plants in the
spring garden. My reference books tell me that they are named
after Euphorbus, physician to the King of Mauretania, a country
in north-west Africa, which lies mostly in the Sahara Desert, so
it is not surprising that they will flourish in poor, dry soil. The
best known is the **Poinsettia** (*Euphorbia pulcherrima*) , which
we can only grow as a house-plant, but there are many hardier
ones. Some of these are evergreen shrubs and others deciduous
perennials dying down in the winter. Like the Poinsettia, they
have brightly coloured leaf bracts, which resemble flowers,
whereas the actual flowers are small and insignificant.
The largest evergreen variety is *E. **characias***, which forms a
handsome bushy shrub about three feet tall, with numerous
stems thickly furnished with narrow green leaves and
terminating in a cluster of small lime-green flowers, each with a
chocolate coloured eye. The closely related *E. c. **wulfenii*** has
blue-green leaves and brighter green-gold flowers. Both open in
April and remain in flower for three to four months after which
the flowering stems die back as fresh ones develop. *E. **robbiae***
looks rather similar, but suckers and is somewhat invasive,
although a splendid plant for a dry, shady corner provided that
you control it. The fascinating *E. **myrsinites*** sprawls flat on the
ground and has the bluest leaves and very bright lime-green
flowers.

Among the herbaceous varieties *E. griffithii* **'Fireglow'** is a
most spectacular plant, resembling a Poinsettia, as the flower
bracts open in May a vivid orange-red fading to green later in
the summer. It increases by suckering to form large, stiff
clumps about three feet high. The more compact *E.*
polychroma develops into a neat bush about 18 inches high with
rounded heads of bright green-gold flowers, a real splash of
sunshine in the distance. Both should be cut to the ground as
they die back in autumn.

All these undemanding plants are well worth growing. They will give you a long period of bright colour as well as attractive foliage and will thrive in a position where few other plants would do as well.

⌁ HELLEBORES ⌁

PERHAPS the most essential attribute of any good garden plant is its staying power, and the length of time it will contribute to your overall picture. I will try to make a few suggestions on what to plant in different seasons, which will reward you with a long-lasting display.

For the winter and early spring I would immediately think of Hellebores. All are evergreen with handsome pinnate leaves, and there are many different species and hybrids. If you grew them all you would probably have continuous flower from Christmas to May. As they are woodland plants, they prefer semi-shaded positions and will tolerate quite a lot of drying in summer, so they are ideal for the base of a wall, providing it is not facing south or south-west. They appreciate a well-drained soil with leaf mould or peat and will seed freely if well established and happy.

Many of them have green flowers, perhaps not the most exciting colour, but look at them closely and you will find a central boss of coloured stamens, and often lovely, pink or purple markings.

The earliest to flower is the well-known and loved **Christmas Rose** – *Helleborus niger*. It is not, however, the easiest to grow. Its white flowers can be splashed by rain and mud, and are much loved by snails and slugs.

The next to flower is *H. lividus* with strange and handsome dark purplish flowers that last for months and dark green leaves with purple markings. It is followed by a close relation, *H. argutifolius* (syn. *H. corsicus*), which is a taller plant and carries its large green flowers on many branching stems.

Best of all is a cross between these two, called *H.x sternii* ***'Boughton Beauty'***, combining the colour of *H. lividus* with the stronger constitution and handsome upright growth of *H. argutifolius.* Definitely a treasure. I find it comes true from seed.

Our native hellebore – *H. foetidus* has smaller green flowers hanging in clusters and finely cut leaves. It tends to be biennial, but seeds very freely.

Finally comes *H. orientalis*, the **Lent Rose**, with the most handsome leaves of all, and flowers closely resembling a Christmas Rose, which come in a wide range of colours from greenish white to dark purple. My own personal preference is for the white ones, which show up so well in a dark corner of the early spring garden.

✑ GROW YOUR OWN TOMATO PLANTS ✍

FOR most of us amateur gardeners, March means the start of the gardening year and we probably begin by thinking we ought to be putting in a few seeds, and particularly vegetable seeds. If you do grow tomatoes, there is a lot to be said for raising your own plants and you can then try out different varieties.

Tomatoes and **peppers** need quite a high temperature to germinate and I find the best place to start them off is the airing cupboard. I use the little flat disks called Jiffy pots, which expand when soaked in water into tiny peat pots enclosed in fine mesh net. One seed goes in each, and I stack the pots in polythene boxes covered with silver foil, so there is no fear of compost getting on to the clean washing. Germination starts in four or five days and it is then essential to examine these every morning and take out those that have sprouted, transferring them to another box on a warm window-sill. Check that the remainder do not dry out, and if any have failed to germinate after ten or twelve days, pop in another seed and start again. This is very economical of expensive seeds. A packet lasts me several years and I always get about 90% germination.

I grow two varieties of tomato – the *F.I. hybrid* **Shirley**, an early and prolific cropper for greenhouse growbags, and a dwarf bush variety called **Pixie**, which is equally good indoors or outdoors and requires very little support. This makes it ideal for pots, which can start in the greenhouse and go outside later on.

Peppers need the same treatment, so they are all sown together about the third week in March.

The little plants stay in their peat pots and the roots are never disturbed, but when these start to come through the netting, they will need re-potting into four-inch pots. They will have to stay on the windowsill for some weeks unless you have a heated greenhouse. An excellent idea I have tried out is to construct a solarium for them out of a cardboard carton – it should be at least 12 inches deep. Cut off the lid and then cut away one of the longer sides to within about two inches from the base and line all the inside surfaces with tin foil. This reflects the light and the seedlings will grow up straight rather than leaning forward to look out of the window. You should also cut a piece of transparent polythene a little wider than the box and long enough to cover the top and hang down in front. Attach a tin cane to this front end to weight it down, and attach the other end to the back of the carton. You can then roll it back like a blind in the day time, but cover up your solarium at night to retain the heat.

I start off **courgettes** and **cucumbers** by the same method, but they go in much later towards the end of April, as they are so fast growing that otherwise they will have outgrown their pots before it is safe to plant them out late in May.

❧ GREY AND SILVER ❧

IF we are embarking on a series of hot, dry summers, thanks either to the greenhouse effect or indeed to one of those climatic swings, which have occurred regularly ever since the Ice Age, we will need to concentrate on plants which have adapted to these conditions.

One group of such plants of great garden value is those with grey or silver leaves. They may seem confusing until you get to know them, but with a few exceptions, they belong to three families, and without exception, they like good drainage and all the sunshine they can get. It follows that in our uncertain climate, many are short-lived and will not survive cold winters, particularly cold, wet winters. They make up for this by growing very fast, so that a tiny plant in spring will make quite a good show by late summer.

This applies particularly to the ***Helichrysums***. I expect most people know *H. **petiolare*** (syn. *petiolatum*) with its round, grey leaves carried on arching sprays, which is such a good plant in tubs and hanging baskets. It can survive out of doors in mild winters, but has only done so once or twice with me, after which it climbed eight or nine feet up a wall, and flowered. You can, of course, over winter it in a heated greenhouse, but the wisest plan is to take cuttings in late summer (and keep them on a window-sill) or in early spring if you still have an old plant. They root very easily.

Two other *Helichrysums* are longer lived. *H. italicum* (syn. *angustifolium*), the **Curry plant**, makes a shapely little bush of needle-like silver grey leaves, which do smell strongly of curry; and *H. splendidum*, another little shrub whose tiny grey leaves grow in clusters, are really quite hardy. Both benefit from an annual trim in spring, but should never be cut back in autumn.

The ***Artemisias*** are made of sterner stuff, and the majority are hardy, particularly the herbaceous ones. All are worthwhile plants. Of the herbaceous ones, two of the most attractive are *A. schmidtiana*, a small, feathery cushion of palest grey green, and *A. stelleriana* of creeping habit, whose prostrate stems are thickly covered with finely cut silver leaves. These both die down in winter; but there are small shrubs among the *Artemisias* too. The most striking is *A. arborescens*, particularly *A.* **'Powis Castle'** (syn. *A. arborescens 'Brass Band'*), which forms a really lovely fast growing silver shrub. *A. absinthium* **'Lambrook Silver'** is another good one. Most beautiful of all is *A. alba 'Canescens'*, a little bush of such fine foliage that it looks like silver filigree. And there are many others. **French Tarragon**, a herb with an unusual flavour that goes so well with chicken, is also an *Artemisia, (A. dracunculus)* needing a dry, sunny situation to flourish.

The third family, the ***Senecios***, includes the largest shrub, *S. greyi*, which forms quite a big, rounded bush, covered in mid-summer with bright yellow daisy flowers. It needs trimming to keep it in good shape. *S. cineraria* **'White Diamond'** is somewhat smaller and less hardy, with finely cut silver leaves. It closely resembles a near relation, *S. maritimus*, which is often grown from seed as a bedding plant, but can also be treated as a perennial. There is also a delightful sprawler, *S. leucostachys*, with a pleasant habit of weaving its way in and out of other plants.

❧ HOW GREEN IS YOUR GARDEN ❧

AS we all try to face up to green problems, the sound of an organic garden becomes very attractive. I do feel that we should aim at cutting down on the use of pesticides, though personally I should find it hard to manage without slug-bait, or an occasional attack on green or black fly! I use a pyrethrum-based spray such as Sprayday or Picket which are said to be harmless to anything except aphids.

The question of fertilisers is rather more complex. Plants obtain their nourishment in very different ways to us humans, or to the animal kingdom. They can manufacture carbohydrates and proteins from the chemicals in air and water, and need only a small proportion from the soil. But for satisfactory plant growth in soil, two things are necessary – humus to improve the texture and the chemicals the plant needs. It is a mistake to suppose that loads of manure or compost will solve all problems and that chemicals or fertilisers will then be unnecessary. Both manure and compost are "man-made" in stable, cow-shed or garden heap, just as fertilisers are in a factory, and all come from natural sources. In a truly "natural" soil in the wild, nothing would be available to plants beyond a few animal droppings. The humus in untilled soil would come from rotting vegetation, and the plant life it supported would be specially adapted to that type of soil and the chemicals it happened to contain.

In order to grow a rich variety of plants, and particularly vegetables and fruit, we have to improve soil texture with humus which will break it up, help it to retain moisture and enable roots to penetrate. By digging in manure or compost as your humus you are adding some chemicals at the same time. Peat or spent mushroom compost give you practically none. But if you continued for years to dig in loads of manure alone, you could well end up with a sick and unbalanced soil, although the texture might be perfect. In the same way, if you use nothing but garden compost and your soil is deficient in some chemical, this compost will be made from plants deficient in the same chemical and therefore cannot supply it to your soil.

The three chemicals, which all plants need for healthy growth are nitrogen, phosphate and potash. I understand that, chemically speaking, it makes no difference to a plant's growth if it obtains its phosphate from bone-meal or superphosphate, although bone-meal breaks down more slowly in the soil; but you do need to use some general fertiliser, be it Growmore, or Blood, Fish and Bone, to get the most from both flower and vegetable gardens.

❧ GROUND COVER FOR ROSE BEDS ❧

I wonder how many people would agree with me that rose-beds, however healthy their occupants, can be very boring at many time of the year. How dull it would be to have a garden with nothing but roses, but equally how dull to have a garden without roses! Nothing else could fill the gap left by these wonderful plants with their long season of flowering, diversity of form and colour and exquisite scent. How should we use them to the best advantage in our own gardens? To climb up wall certainly, if we have walls, or perhaps trained up a pillar or pergola, but how much more effective then to have a *clematis* scrambling up through them and flowering either in a contrasting or a complementary colour. Care should be taken to choose a late-flowering variety (the *C.'Jackmanii'* types) which are cut back hard in early spring, or you will find it impossible to prune the rose without cutting back the clematis and thus losing all its crop of flowers for that summer.

In mixed borders I personally think that roses look at their best either singly, in the case of old-fashioned or **shrub roses**, or in groups of two or three of the same variety if you are planting **hybrid teas** or **floribundas**. They will associate well with all but the most rampant of herbaceous plants, although you should be careful not to plant anything tall in front or them.

If you have a formal bed, particularly if it is in constant view of your windows, consider planting the centre with roses (again all one variety would look best) leaving room round the edges for low-growing shrubs, ***Potentilla*** perhaps, and ***Hebes***, and silver and grey plants, and then underplant the roses with ***violas***.

Violas would definitely be included in any list of plants, which flower over a long period. I started with half a dozen plants some years ago, and have never needed to buy more as they seed freely. Some always live through the winter, and then start flowering in May, and by the time the roses come out the new seedlings are flowering as well and the whole bed is solid with their little faces, with the roses flowering above. The original plants are white, and the majority still run true although I allow a few blue ones, and I pull out any that revert to a colour that I don't like. By the end of August they are getting a bit tatty and if you cut them back they will go on flowering all the autumn. I also have a few plants of the delightful *V. cornuta*, with smaller and more delicate flowers on rather longer stems, like a cloud of tiny white or blue butterflies. They are basically perennials and will go on from year to year if happy and well-established. I think they need good drainage as they seem to die out in ground level beds, but do well in a raised one, trailing down over the retaining wall.

✂ TULIPS ✂

NOTHING can quite replace the tulip in the May garden. Its long-lasting flowers on their stiff stems defy the weather, and a few groups among the fresh green shoots of the herbaceous perennials will add interest and colour to any mixed border.

I have never personally felt very enthusiastic about them when massed as bedding plants, and have no particular wish to visit the Dutch bulb fields, but cleverly used they can transform any garden during the rather difficult period when everything is full of promised, but performance lags behind.

The tulip has always been a much-loved flower. Most of the wild species come from Asia Minor, from Turkey, Iran and the Caucasus, and they inspired many of the decorative patterns in the art of Islam. In the 17th century they were introduced into Europe, and a wave of Tulipmania started in Holland, hybridisation began and the rich man would pay the equivalent of hundreds of pounds for a bulb. Even those streaked and mottled with white (which we now know is caused by a virus disease) were highly prized.

The little wild tulips are charming. Most of them flower in April. Best known is *T. Kaufmanniana*, the water-lily tulip, with its spotted leaves, which has now been hybridised, and has many different named varieties. I am particularly fond of *T. clusiana*, the delicate pink and white lady tulip, and there are very many others. They only flourish in full sun, where their bulbs will dry out and bake during the summer. This is really true of all tulips, and ideally they should be lifted when they finish flowering, and the bulbs stored in a dry place. This is not really necessary if they are grown in a well-drained and sunny border, and planted deep enough. A quick guide to planting any bulbs is to plant the top with twice its own height in soil above it. For tulips this should be at least four inches, so you need a six-inch hole. The dead foliage of tulips is said to cause disease, so you should clear it away completely as soon as it withers, and then mark the place where they are planted.

We now have a multitude of lovely colours and shapes to

choose from among the May-flowering bedding tulips. I love the lily-flowered ones especially white *T. 'Triumphator'* and also the fascinating *T.* **'Groenland'** (syn. *T.* 'Greenlands'), which is pink with green markings, and its white and green companion *T.* **'Spring Green'**.

One of the best ways to admire and study them is to visit the West Parterre garden at Hatfield House.

⊀ OSMANTHUS AND EXOCHORDAS ⅋

TWO early flowering shrubs have been particularly lovely this spring. Both usually flower in May, but some years are about a month earlier, and then last well through the cold weather in April.

I have grown *Osmanthus delavayi* for a long time and it is one of my favourite shrubs. It was collected in north-west China in the last century by Père Delavay, one of the intrepid French missionary priests to whom we own so many good garden plants. Both he and Père David (who also has a deer named after him) risked their lives plant-hunting in the remoter parts of China and many plants bear their names. The *Osmanthus* has small, dark green, holly-like leaves and forms a dense bush wreathed in sweetly scented small white tubular flowers in April and May. It can grow quite tall, up to about five feet, but can also be kept shorter by regular pruning after flowering. It seems happy in sun or semi-shade and it is worthwhile to plant it beside a path where you can catch the perfume as you pass.

Exochordas also come from north-west China and since a particularly good clone called *E. x macrantha* **'The Bride'** has been on the market it has become very popular. The Bride is very free-flowering and has a graceful weeping habit. Once you have seen one covered with its large white flowers on slender stems you feel it is a must. It is deciduous and delicate pale green leaves come out with the flowers. It grows quickly into quite a large shrub, but can be pruned after flowering to keep its shape.

Although *Exochordas* are said to prefer a sunny position, mine does well in semi-shade, and I have planted a late flowering *clematis* to grow up into it and provide colour and interest later in the summer.

✤ YOU MUST HAVE SOME ANNUALS ✤

IT is fashionable now to rather decry annuals, and to say "I want a trouble-free garden, so I am concentrating on shrubs", and it is certainly true that to "bed-out" twice a year in any part of the garden is expensive both in time and money – even if you raise your own plants which will take up more of your time! But that approach misses out on both sheets of colour and the varied effects which only annuals can provide.

I have long ago stopped growing **wallflowers** (*Erysimum ercheiri*); instead I have a sheet of self-sown **forget-me-nots** (*Myosotis*) in many parts of the garden each spring. Start with a few plants, and try to get them a good deep blue colour, and then allow them to colonise among shrubs (they look wonderful with **azaleas**) or among herbaceous plants, and particularly where you have groups of **tulips**. Pull them out as soon as they finish flowering in June, but leave a few to seed. After a few years you have to be fairly firm about clearing and thinning the seedlings in the autumn to stop them from choking the other plants.

I like to follow on with **tobacco plants** (*Nicotiana*) in many places. These do need to be raised from seed each year but are very easy to deal with. **Busy Lizzies** (*Impatiens walleriana*) are another stand-by, happy in shade and flowering away well into the autumn. They are tricky from seed and fairly expensive to buy, but root easily from cuttings. If you take these in autumn and keep them on a window-sill through the winter you will have your own plants the following spring.

Most other annuals are more easily looked after in tubs or large flower-pots. I love *petunias* and must have a few each year. *Trailing lobelia* (*Lobelia erinus cultivars*) too, will spill over the edge of a container, perhaps one in which you also plant an upright *fuchsia* or a **geranium** (*pelargonium*). They will do much better in pots if the summer is wet.

⚜ PLANTING IN CONTAINERS ⚜

IN May we are perhaps thinking about how we plan to plant up tubs, pots, window boxes or other garden containers, and it is fun to try something a little more adventurous or maybe ring the changes.

My first consideration would always be a colour scheme and to choose plants which will give a long-lasting display. Another factor is where you intend to place them. *Fuchsias* are invaluable for their long flowering qualities, but do need a lot of water and some shade, whereas *petunias* and **geraniums** need as much sunshine as you can give them.

If you can over-winter your containers in a cold greenhouse, you should not need to re-plant them every year, but I would always recommend knocking out the plants and re-potting with fresh compost each spring when the plants are starting into growth. They can go back into the same containers, but need a fresh supply of nourishment. I also think it is important to feed them regularly – at least every fortnight – I use Phostrogen in my watering can. Remember too, that very little rainwater will soak through the foliage even in the heaviest downpour, so they will need very regular watering throughout the summer.

I now have two very large earthenware tubs, too heavy to move above, so I grow the plants in large plastic pots to drop into them. For the spring I plant early **tulips** and **forget-me-nots** (*Myosotis*). These come from the greenhouse as the flowers are opening, and then I substitute two large *fuchsias* which have also over-wintered in the greenhouse.

Other plants which have over-wintered are ***Campanula isophylla***, which seems to tolerate a shady corner in the summer, and several more *fuchsias*. I find these combine very well with perennial **verbenas**. I take cuttings of these every year. For hot, sunny positions, I grow a variety of ***ivy-leafed geraniums***. Of these, the small single-flowered ones known as **"Austrian window-box"** are far the most free-flowering and stand up well to wet weather. They seem to do best if several are crammed together in the same container.

A rather unusual plant which enjoys hot sunshine is the delightful little blue ***Convolvulus sabatius*** (syn. *C. mauritanicus*), and one could also try the silver-leafed *C. cneorum*. Neither of these is a climber. *Ipomoea* or **Morning Glory** definitely does best for me if grown in a pot, and then allowed to climb up a wall, preferably through a **rose**, or other climbing shrub.

⨍ HOSTAS ⨎

JUNE is such a month for flowers everywhere that it may seem a surprising time to write about plants which are valued above all for their fascinating leaves. Perhaps it is the recent popularity of foliage house plants which has woken us up to the value of foliage in the garden. *Hostas* or plantain lilies have just unfurled their leaves displaying a rich variation of size and colour and contributing both shape and texture to the summer garden.

They do need a moist rich soil to give of their best and are happiest in partial shade. They also need a bit of elbow room. The leaves spread out to cover quite a large area and don't look their best if other plants jostle them. A corner planted solely with hostas can be a very effective sight; they deserve a place in front of the border but you can plant bulbs around their crowns which will be quite happy hidden under the *hosta* leaves once their own foliage dies down.

The taller, more upright varieties can be grouped behind those with flatter growth and these tend to have the tallest flower spikes. *Hosta* flowers are just as rewarding as the leaves, delicate funnel shaped bells in pale lilac or white on stiff, upright stems.

The first to send its big pointed buds poking out of the ground in spring is *H. crispula* whose large pointed leaves are pale green with broad white margins – *H. undulata var. undulata 'Albomarginata'* (syn. *H.* **'Thomas Hogg'**) is probably the most robust form. His flowers are shorter than the type, so he can be grown in the front row.

H. lancifolia is a tall, upright variety with narrow green leaves and lilac flower spikes. *H. sieboldiana* is the largest and most impressive, with large round blue-green leaves elegantly ribbed, and almost white flowers. Its variety, *H.s. elegans*, has the bluest leaf colour.

Last of mine to appear, so that each year I begin to wonder if it has died during the winter, is *H. fortunei* *'Albopicta'*. It has fascinating markings and is another for the front. The young leaves are bright yellow with green margins and a network of green veins, although later on, as the flowers develop, this variation fades and the leaves turn completely green.

There are many other varieties, too. A favourite one is *H. undulata var. univittata*, well-named, as its leaves are green splashed with white, and twisted – in fact, they undulate. *H.* **'Halcyon'** is very dwarf, later flowering and with very blue leaves.

A word of warning – do be generous with the slug pellets around your *hostas* in the spring. Once holes are nibbled in the young leaves the whole effect of your plant will be ruined for the year. I am told that the organic solution is to use oyster grit, or crushed eggshells round the plants in early spring.

⚘ IRISES ⚘

TALL bearded irises are at their stately best in June. They don't really show to advantage jostling with their neighbours in a mixed border, but in the right setting they are superb. Though their flowering season is short their tall sword-like leaves add interest and texture all summer. They only succeed in a sunny place and like to have their rhizomes half uncovered to bake in the sun. Ideally they should be lifted, split up and replanted every few years after they have finished flowering. I find this hard to achieve as time is short and the ground is hard in July. So my few clumps have to take their chance – with an occasional feed of bone-meal, and don't really flower as they should.

The family of Irises is enormous, and very varied in its likes and dislikes. The root systems take many forms and are a guide as to where the plants would prefer to grow. In early spring we can enjoy the dwarf bulbous irises, *I. reticulata* and *I. histrioides*, which can be treated like any other spring bulbs, planted in autumn and left undisturbed year after year. Their choice is for well-drained partial shade. In this group too, are the Dutch irises of the florist trade.

All irises with rhizomes or tubers like sunny, well-drained positions. The tall bearded ones have many smaller relations, most of which flower in May. They originate in hot countries such as Greece. Best known are the many hybrid forms of *I. pumila*. They vary in height from three to ten inches and are available in a great variety of colours in all shade of purple, blue and yellow. They are quite delightful in the front of a sunny border and increase with great speed if happy. Preferring a limey soil, they thrive on generous amount of bone-meal.

Another large group includes all the grassy-leafed and fibrous rooted irises, which enjoy a lot of moisture and will tolerate shade. Some, like our native **flag irises** and the Japanese *I. kaempferi* and *I. laevigata* varieties are almost water plants, liking to grow on the edge of ponds and streams. You can make them happy in a boggy or badly drained part of the garden. *I. Sibirica* will tolerate rather dryer conditions and is handsome in any border, and there are delightful smaller varieties like the curious black and green **Widow Iris**, and, my favourite of all, which I call the **Plum Iris**. It smells strongly of ripe fruit, and has flowers coloured like the bloom on a purple plum and is, I think, *I. graminea*.

I. foetidissima is happy in any shady corner and is most eye-catching in autumn with handsome orange seed-heads. The variegated form is particularly attractive. Its stiff foliage is evergreen and is quite a feature in the winter garden. In winter too, we can enjoy the fragile flowers of *I. stylosa*.

The *Iris* family is truly one for all seasons.

☆ KEEPING BORDERS COLOURFUL ✍

HERBACEOUS plants brighten our gardens in June, so it is well worth giving a little thought as to which will give us the longest period in flower, and how we can prolong this. Some of the best loved are over all too quickly. *Paeonies* are among the most beautiful of all flowers, and although their flowers are short-lived the young red shoots are also delightful and the leaves so handsome that they continue to look well all the summer. Not so **Oriental poppies** (*Papaver orientale*) which die back after flowering, leaving a dreary gap in the border. **Lupins** (*Lupinus*) present the same problem. Care should be taken to plant something, such as a hardy *fuchsia* in front of them, or to have some colourful annuals ready to fill the gap.

Delphiniums are among the most spectacular of plants, and although their glory is short-lived they will flower again in the autumn if you cut them down, leaves and all, as they finish flowering, give them a good feed of general fertiliser and water well if the ground is dry.

Alchemillas should also be cut down, and although they may not have much of a second flowering they will quickly grow a fresh crop of their charming pale green frilly leaves.

Campanulas, however, are another story, particularly the tall C. *persicifolia* (the **peach-leafed bell-flower**). They will flower throughout the summer if you take the trouble to cut off the dead flower spikes. This is also a worthwhile precaution to stop them seeding all over the garden. The even taller C. *lactiflora* (the **milky bell-flower**) is another wonderful plant, but will probably need staking to give of its best. Their shorter cousins, the dwarf creeping *campanulas* are also invaluable in front of the border, or to tuck into odd corners.

Many other less well-known plants have long flowering periods.

Among them *Tradescantia* (the spiderwort) opens its blue flowers for months on end. Look for a good deep blue, some of the paler ones are a bit wishy-washy. If happy in semi-shade the charming *Astrantias* last well, and for later in the year in a sunny border, the best **Michaelmas Daisy** is *Aster x frikartii* which produces its large single mauve-blue daises from August to October.

❧ FASHIONS IN PLANTS ❧

Gardeners are often very fashion conscious and we are constantly tempted to try out new plants which we have read about or seen in other people's gardens. Some prove their worth and become well-known and generally available, others are quickly forgotten.

The *Diascias* are a good example of a worthwhile plant. They come from South Africa and few people had heard of them ten years ago. Now they are an invaluable addition to our gardens from June onwards. They are not fully hardy and require a sunny well-drained position to survive the winter, but will then quickly spread over quite a large area. Their delightful sprays of small pink flowers cover the plants for months.

The lovely daisy-flowered *Osteospermums* also from South Africa, survive some winters in well-drained soil, and a few varieties are quite hardy. They have been around for quite a long time, but the new varieties, which constantly appear are only half-hardy and it is wise to take cuttings every autumn and over-winter them in a greenhouse. They root very easily. I particularly enjoy the prostrate one *O. ecklonis*, whose white flowers open in the sun, with blue centres, and close showing the metallic purple-blue backs of the petals.

I wonder if one of the latest "fashion" plants, the **Cerinthe**, will also establish itself. They come from Southern Greece and have the old name of **honeywort**, so I suppose they have been around for some time, but few people grew them until recently. They are easy to germinate from seed and will self-sow quite prolifically in the right place. Their blue-green leaves and strange purple flowers are fascinating, but they do straggle about and flop forward. So again a sunny position, good drainage and in the front of the border.

Another "new" plant I wouldn't be without is the blue *Corydalis flexuosa* from China, which flowers in early spring. The delicate leaves appear in February or March and disappear in early summer soon after the flowers fade. They appreciate a damp soil with plenty of humus and will be happy in shade. As will another recent introduction, the creeping *Veronica peduncularis* **'Georgia Blue'**. This is a wonderful plant, very easy to please and forms great mats of dark leaves with bronze tints covered with bright blue star-like flowers in April and May.

◁ CLEMATIS ▷

I think I get more interest and pleasure from my *clematis* than any other summer flowering plants. They look so very bedraggled and dead throughout the winter that it is impossible to imagine those thin, lifeless stems can develop into such a marvellous burst of large colourful flowers. They need very little room for this display since they are at their happiest climbing up and decorating roses or other shrubs; or they will cover a wall if you give them a few wires to cling to; but they are capricious plants, and if you don't treat them properly they will sulk and probably die on you.

The original planting is all important. You should dig a hole at least one foot deep and one foot in diameter, and fill it with good compost, or your own soil well enriched with compost or well-rotted manure. Take the clematis carefully out of its pot (probably better to cut the pot away, rather than risk damaging the root ball). Spread out the tangled roots carefully and put the plant in your hole with the stem junction just below the surface. Cover the roots generously with peat and a handful of bone-meal, and fill in the soil, firming by hand rather than stamping it in.

Clematis are perfectly hardy, but do demand a cool root run, plenty of moisture and an adequate diet. Young plants probably get wilt disease and die more from lack of water than anything else. When I went round the famous gardens at Treasure's Nursery I noticed that their *clematis* were all planted in open-ended lengths of drainpipe protecting the stems, and I have done this successfully ever since. I use odd lengths of black plastic drainpipe, abut six inches in diameter and four inches deep, which I slip down over the plants before filling in, leaving about an inch of rim protruding above the soil. Apart from protecting the roots I think the dual benefit is that you can be sure that any water or liquid fertiliser goes into the roots rather than running away over the soil, and I do water frequently with Phostrogen in the spring and early summer. Flat pieces of stone over the root area will also help to conserve moisture but lift and replace them when you mulch in early spring.

Of course, if you want a *clematis* to climb up a tree or a shrub you must plant it a little distance away, or it will never get enough moisture – and give it a bamboo cane to lead it into the host plant. It is really more satisfactory to plant both at the same time. And do remember that all clematis will be tempted to grow away towards the light, so that you may have to keep coaxing the young shoots back into position when they are growing fast in May and June.

However carefully you plant your *clematis* they will continue to need love and attention to give of their best and avoid the dreaded wilt disease. This is caused by a fungus attacking the stems and normally only affects the large-flowered hybrids. A fungicide spray such as Benlate early in the season may give protection, but it is now generally thought that the main cause is dryness at the roots. *Clematis*, particularly young plants, need copious watering in dry seasons. A good mulch in early spring will also help.

Finally, there is the question of pruning. A good rule of thumb is to remember that the later the clematis flowers, the more pruning it requires. All *clematis* should be pruned back to a pair of buds about twelve inches from the ground the first spring after planting. Thereafter, those that flower in early spring (**Montanas** and **Alpinas**) need no further pruning unless you want to reduce their size, in which case, prune back after flowering.

Those with large flowers that bloom in May and June should be cut back to three feet the second year and then only need tidying up, shortening the stems to the top pair of buds in February or March.

Those that flower from July onwards all flower on the new wood made in the same year. They should be cut back to within a foot from the ground the second year and then each year to within three feet. In practice these are much the easiest to deal with, particularly if you want to grow them through **roses** or other shrubs, as after you have cleared out all the top growth, *even if it is covered with lovely fat buds*, you can then prune or tidy up the host plant.

The azalea bed

August: Clematis 'Alba Luxurians'and clematis 'John Huxtable', white hydrangea and busy lizzies with camomile growing between the paving stones.

Early August: White Iceberg rose grown as a shrub; gypsophila 'Rosy Veil'; verbena 'Loveliness'; and pink and white phlox. A potentilla and violas grow on the ground level bed.

Blue convolvulus, white petunias and silver foliage grow in a collection of pots of different sizes in a sunny corner. The tallest one is an old chimney pot. This idea is sometimes called a potscape.

⋊ COLOUR FOR AUGUST ⋉

AUGUST can be quite a difficult month in the garden, as **roses** take a rest and the prodigal flowers of June and July die down leaving big gaps in borders. I will try to suggest a few ideas to help.

For vivid colour nothing is more useful than the border *phlox*. Provided that they get enough moisture in dry weather they never fail to put up a good show. Planted in front of *delphiniums* or **lupins** they will take over when these are cut back after flowering. *Delphiniums* will flower again in the autumn if they are cut right down to the grounds, leaves and all, watered well and given a handful of Growmore or other general purpose fertiliser. By that time the phloxes will be over and can be cut back in their turn.

Actaea (syn. *Cimicifuga*) or **snake-root** is a really elegant herbaceous plant that flowers late. It has handsome pinnate leaves and the flowers are creamy white tassels, four or five inches in length and carried at right angles to the stems in a curious and unusual manner. Planted with a clump of *delphiniums* it will help to supply height when they are cut down.

Eupatorium is another late flowering plant, which I admire at the back of a wide border. It has flat, pinkish purple flowers, grows up to six feet high in good soils and likes partial shade.

More tall spikes are provided by an August flowering bulb, *Galtonia*, the summer hyacinth. Pale green stems carry large greenish white bells, and once established they seed freely. It is a useful thing to plant among early flowering shrubs.

I am fond of the ornamental thistles, and the delightful biennial, *Eryngium giganteum*, **Miss Willmott's Ghost**, is a most

41

attractive plant. The spiky silver-blue ruffs, which surround the darker blue centres of the flowers, have an almost ghostly appearance in evening light.

Another very attractive member of the thistle family is *Echinops ritro*, a really tall plant with completely round flower heads, like little blue hedgehogs on tall stems. The leaves rather resemble the globe **artichoke**, but are dark green rather than silver. Why not have a group of artichokes in the herbaceous border? The leaves are as handsome as the flower buds are delicious to eat!

◁ SAVING WATER ▷

MY soil is well drained and dries out all too quickly, so I am always trying to work out what can be done to keep everything growing happily.

We all know that the Rolls Royce solution is to dig in lots of humus and cover everything with a thick mulch. The theory is excellent, but not easy to achieve in a garden of any size; so priority should be given to the plants which need it most. **Roses** and **clematis** come high on this list, particularly the latter, which suffer badly from wilt or die back if they are short of moisture. Covering their roots with a stone helps to conserve this and I try to give mine a full can of water every week with liquid feed in it. It is always better to give plants a really good soak at intervals than a little water more often. If you need to plant something in dry weather, be sure to soak the root ball first and to pour water into the hole and let it soak in before installing the plant.

I have tried mixing some of the new moisture retaining gel, P.4. in my potting compost. Some garden writers are enthusiastic about it, others more doubtful, but I hope it will help. It is quite expensive.

In the vegetable garden, the old system of keeping the hoe going in dry weather and creating a fine tilth which will conserve any moisture underneath, is probably the best plan. I have also tried sinking plastic funnels between the plants, made from plastic bottles with the tops and bottoms cut off, and holes punched in the sides. I filled these funnels with small stones to prevent them getting clogged up with soil. Clay pots sunk into the ground are another alternative. I hope that by watering into these, rather than wetting the top layer of soil I shall do more good to my **courgettes**, **peas**, **beans** and **tomatoes**, than by surface watering.

⚜ BLENDING COLOURS ⚜

JUNE and July are the months when we all expect our gardens to be at their most colourful, so I thought I would write about my ideas on colour. It is said that everyone sees colours differently, and I personally really dislike red and yellow together in the garden as well as anywhere else; but I find the third primary colour, blue, is the great catalyst that enhances and pulls together all the other colours. Think of a white or pale yellow colour scheme and add a little touch of soft blue, or of one of the red or purples lit up with a blue that has a touch of mauve in it.

Yellow to my mind is the colour to be most careful about. We all rejoice at the sight of **daffodils** (*Narcissus*), but they look their best surrounded and isolated by green grass. Many silvery plants have stiff and uncompromising yellow daisy flowers. I cut them off, though I can just accept them on *Senecio greyi*, as the colour is a little softer than the others, and its flowers open in an exuberant burst. The big *Phlomis fruticosa* (**Jerusalem Sage**) with its lovely silvery leaves is a joy, but I am always glad when its yellow flowers change to rather charming grey-green seed heads. As an exception, I love lime-green, and could have **Alchemilla mollis** foaming about everywhere in June. In fact, I do, as once you have it in the garden it seeds itself enthusiastically and you have to be ruthless to keep it in check. The leaves are so pretty too; it is one of my favourite plants.

It is quite a good approach to think of gardening as if you were painting a picture – that is, of course, exactly what you are doing, and excitingly it is a picture that changes all the time. So you have to think about both form and colour as you plant. Think about **azaleas** if you are lucky enough to have an acid soil. They can scream at each other if you are not careful to keep the pinks away from the bright yellows and oranges. Or think of **Hybrid Tea** or *floribunda* roses all together in a bed. I don't really like mixed rose beds and prefer them planted in blocks of colour which harmonise. It is said that no flower colours clash, but I can't really agree. Green is, of course, the harmony that we take for granted, and grey or silver foliage will soften any plant grouping. Yellow foliage is lovely in the winter, but in summer I feel that it makes the plant look unhealthy, and might be better used discreetly in the background to lighten up dark corners.

❧ HARDY GERANIUMS ❧

WHEN we talk of *geraniums*, we are usually thinking of *pelargoniums*, the non-hardy varieties that give us so much colour and interest all summer long in greenhouses or outdoors in pots or containers. The true geraniums or **cranesbills** are fully hardy and one of the great standbys in our flower borders. They die down in winter and reappear as large clumps, with pretty parasol-shaped leaves, which flower continuously from early summer onwards. They make wonderful ground cover, smothering weeds and associating well with roses or flowering shrubs. They come in many good colours and prefer a sunny position, but will grow in partial shade and in any garden soil.

Our native wild form is *G. pratense* with saucer-shaped clear blue flowers. This is quite handsome enough to be a border plant, but is tall and inclined to flop. The best blue for gardens is *G.* **'Johnsons's Blue'**, which has shorter and neater growth. *G. wallichianum* 'Buxton's Variety' (syn. **'Buxton's Blue'**) is also invaluable as it flowers later in the season from July to October. A healthy plant of this will cover an area about three feet wide, but as it does not appear above the ground until May you can plant bulbs or early spring plants round it, which will not mind being covered up later on. It looks splendid hanging over a wall, but should otherwise be planted in front of the border.

MY favourite of all the herbaceous geraniums is from Nepal. This is a really lovely plant and beautiful with **Iceberg roses**. It disappears completely in winter, and comes up in April to form large clumps about 18 inches tall covered with delicate white flowers in June and July. But it is invasive and spreads out rapidly in good soil. I find I have to dig it up in autumn and split the clumps, replanting with a smaller piece, about every other year.

The *G. endresii* are a useful family. They have shining silvery-pink flowers and they also increase rapidly. They seed freely, often crossing with other geraniums so that you often get a colour mix of pink, mauve and white, making very effective ground cover. I am less fond of *G. phaeum*, the earliest to flower – known also as **The Mourning Widow**, as its rather insignificant flowers are a sombre dark purple. This seeds so prolifically that it can take over, and I now pull up the seedlings as soon as they come into flower. But there are good, rich purples, too. The low-growing *G. sanguineum*, the **Bloody Cranesbill**, has vivid magenta flowers. There is also a white form, and a very pretty dwarf pink one called *G.s. var.* ***striatum*** (syn. *G.s. var. lancastriense*). The tall *G.* ***psilostemo*** is quite spectacular and has bright purple flowers with a dark eye.

Another exquisite plant is *G.* ***renardii***, with pale, almost silvery green leaves and white flowers delicately veined in purple; and the best ground cover is the shell pink flowered G. ***macrorrhizum***, the only one that spreads by rooting systems.

Of the really dwarf varieties, my favourite is *G. cinereum* 'Ballerina', a real gem with large lilac flowers veined in purple. This is only about six inches high and flowers the whole summer. It needs a special place where it can be admired without being smothered by other plants.

There are many other varieties in this invaluable family and it is well worthwhile to grow as many as possible as they all complement each other.

❧ TAKING CUTTINGS ☙

I am often asked about taking cuttings, so with apologies to those who know it all better than I do, I will try to give a few tips.

Firstly, it is a good idea to be ready to deal immediately with any cuttings you may be given. I find a satisfactory plan is to prepare a little bit of ground in the shade, preferably where you could cover it with a pane of glass in the winter. The Rolls Royce solution would be a small cold frame. Get rid of any weeds, fork up the soil and then cover the ground about two to three inches deep with a mixture of peat and sand, and water it well. Then as you insert the cuttings, firm them well in and cover them with a glass coffee or 2 lb. (1 kg) jam jar.

Leave this on until you see growth beginning and then remove the jar, but do not pot them on until they are growing well. Many are best left until the following spring. Never let your ground dry out, but you can easily water over the tops of the jars.

Take great care not to let your cuttings wilt before they go in. Either put them straight into a polythene bag (in a friend's garden) or take a jar of water round with you in your own.

There are three sorts of cuttings (not counting leaf or root cuttings) soft wood, half-ripened wood and hard wood. The first two are taken in spring and summer. For soft wood ones, such as herbaceous plants, cut them off with a sharp knife, just below a leaf joint or node, carefully remove all but the top few leaves and insert them firmly one third buried in your cuttings bed. Use a pencil or dibber to make the holes.

Geraniums are treated in the same way, but it is probably better to put them in round the edge of a flower pot, cover it with a polythene bag and keep them in a cold greenhouse or on the window-sill until they are ready to pot on. They root very easily. You could use the polythene bag method for all summer cuttings, but I find glass jars quicker and easier. If you are using flower-pots I am told it is better to use John Innes No. 1 (with soil in it) rather than a soil-less compost as it is less likely to dry out and you will get sturdier plants.

Half-ripe cuttings are taken in the summer after the side shoots of the plant have begun to harden. You pull them off the stem of the plant with what is called a "heel", so that there is a little bit of stem left on the cuttings. Trim this heel if it is jagged, take off the lower leaves and insert it firmly as before. If possible, choose shoots from the sunny side of the parent plant.

Fuchsias are taken in this way as are most small shrubby plants.

Hard wood cuttings are treated quite differently. They are taken in late autumn but cutting pieces of hardened stem about eight inches long after the leaves have fallen. Cut off the tops, make a small trench and stamp them firmly in with two-thirds of the cuttings below the ground. They will start to grow the following spring, but do not move them until the next autumn. This method works well for **roses** and soft fruit bushes such as **currants** and **gooseberries**.

Oddly enough, cuttings put in close together seem to encourage each other to root, so I always try to put two to three under each jar.

⚜ OLD FAVOURITES ⚜

IF any garden plant has an English name as well as its Latin one, it is quite a good indication that it is completely hardy and has been grown here for a very long time.

Santolina by its old name **Cotton Lavender** may well have been introduced by the Romans, and was extensively grown in medieval gardens, both as a herb and as an alternative to **Box** (*Buxus*) for edging beds and making patterns in Knot Gardens. It is a small bushy shrub, with feathery silver foliage, which will get straggly unless it is kept in check by hand clipping every spring. This will keep it in a neat round shape, and discourage it from producing its not very attractive yellow button flowers.

Another old favourite is **Lambs Ears** – *Stachys byzantina* (syn. *S. lanata*) – a very useful carpeter for dry, sunny places. I rather like the ordinary form with its soft, downy silver leaves and tall floppy flowering stems, but if you want something tidier there is a non-flowering variety called *S.b.* **'Silver Carpet'** which is neater and more compact.

Another carpeter, but a very invasive one is **Snow-In-Summer** (*Cerastium tomentosum*) which will take over a rock garden, smothering other plants if it gets a chance. It also has a less rampant form, *C. t. var.* **columnae**, which is a most attractive plant. It grows slowly as a neat flat mat with almost white foliage, and charming little white flowers.

All these are ever-greys which will keep their foliage in winter, but snow or continuous rain will leave them a bit bedraggled.

❧ POTENTILLA FRUTICOSA ☙

WHEN choosing plants, which have a long flowering season, it is difficult to think of many shrubs, although many of them make up for this with handsome foliage or good autumn colour. There is, however, one small shrub, which remains in flower over quite a long period and is really useful in any garden plan.

Potentilla fruticosa flowers fairly continuously from May onwards, and if cut back when it pauses, it will break into new growth and start again.

There are many different varieties. I prefer the pale yellow or white ones to the rather hot tangerine or red shades, and there is now a very pretty pink one called *P.f.* *'Princess'*. *P.f.* *'Manchu'* (syn. *P. davurica var. mandschurica*) is one of the best whites as it has large flowers for a *potentilla*, and opens its delicate green leaves early in February. It is quite a large bush, as is *P.f.* *'Vilmoriniana'*, which has silver-grey leaves and pale yellow flowers. *P.f.* **'Elizabeth'** has large yellow flowers and is rather more dwarf in habit, as is the pink 'Princess'. I have a dwarf white, which is attractive and useful, but I do not know its name as I rooted it from a cutting I was given.

They seem to be completely hardy and to tolerate any soil or conditions, but do show to advantage in full sun. They root very easily from cuttings taken early in the summer.

❧ PLANTING WIDE MIXED BORDERS ✄

I spend quite a lot of time planning my flower beds to try and achieve a balance of shape and colour throughout the year, so I thought I might encourage others to do the same by describing how I might think of planting a fairly wide border, say 10 feet, with a background of a hedge or, in my case even better, a high wall. If you have a wall, of course, you have the advantage of growing things up it, but what? Certainly not **roses**, which need a lot of attention and will not show their best if plants grow up in front of them. I suggest *Chaenomeles*, or **flowering quince**, which will look lovely in spring. It flowers on bare branches in March and April, and gives you a green background later on. It needs to be pruned hard after flowering, so leave room to get at it, and you could plant *clematis* to grow up through it. I would always choose the late-flowering *C. viticella* type, which you cut right down in winter and, to be successful, I think you must be able to get at the roots to give them water and liquid feed when they start to grow hard in May and June. Before that they will need a good sprinkling of blood, fish and bone, or Growmore, and mulch of manure or compost. *Clematis* are greedy plants.

Towards the back of the border I would plan for two or three tall **shrub roses**. Alternatively, you could plant vigorous *floribundas* such as **Iceberg** and allow them to grow tall. I would certainly want some roses. **Cecile Brunner**, perhaps,

50

further forward, with its succession of tiny delicate pink flowers all the summer, **The Fairy** to spill forward right in front, or **White Pet**. I would like one or two early flowering shrubs towards the back. In my own border I have a *Magnolia stellata* which is growing too big, and a *philadelphus* which fills the garden with its scent in June. I planted a white *clematis viticella* behind it, which after three years is now vigorous enough to climb right over the *philadelphus* and cover it with flowers again in August.

I do enjoy one big clump of *delphiniums*, which I cut down as soon as they have finished flowering, and also a *Crambe* at the back, which sends up a six foot flowering spike of tiny white blossoms in June. In front of them I have *paeonies*, and *phlox* to take over in July and August, and the hardy *fuchsias* for the autumn. It is important to cut each plant back, or dead head it, as it finishes flowering. Right in front, I plant a few patches of annuals, *verbenas*, *petunias* and some taller **tobacco** (*Nicotiana*) or *cosmos* further back. You could also try *alchemilla*, or *violas*, whatever you enjoy. I am always experimenting.

For the winter I have *Euphorbias* and *Iris foetidissima* right back under the wall, and rue and perennial **wallflowers** (*erysimum*); also evergreen further forward, and I plant dwarf early **tulips** where the annuals have been. There are many other plants in my border, perhaps too many, but at least there is not much room left for weeds!

❧ PLANTING NARROW SUNNY BORDERS ❧

I have suggested some ideas for planting a wide border, but

many gardens only have space for much narrow plantings. One thing we all have is some space for growing things against our house walls – which will probably take the form of a narrow border in either sun or shade.

I am thinking of a narrow sunny border facing south or south-west. The soil will probably be poor and dry and need all the humus you can give it. It is helpful to know what plants will tolerate such conditions, and it is often a good idea to find out where they originate. South African or Mediterranean natives are likely to be happy. If you plant **roses** or other climbers on the house walls they will need a deep hole filled with good enriched soil to give them a start. It is a worthwhile idea to plant a late-flowering *clematis* such as **'Perle d'Azur'** to grow into the climber, but it will need regular watering in summer. The larger flowered *clematis* that bloom in May and June are often not so successful. They are more subject to disease and do not need to be cut back during the winter, thus making it difficult to prune and tie in the climber. These are best grown on their own on a trellis, and will need some shade on their roots.

For the rest of the planting, small bulbs, *crocus*, *scilla* or **dwarf tulips** will give you colour in spring. I would also plant *Nerines* at the back against the wall. They should increase quickly and give you a lovely display of pink flowers in the autumn. I have them under the window in my courtyard and have to thin them out, or the whole bed would be covered with their long strap-like leaves in early summer, smothering other plants. These leaves die back in August leaving rather a gap. I am now thinking of combining them with blue *Agapanthus*, another South African member of the **lily** family, which flowers earlier and keeps its handsome dark green leaves until the winter.

I always want silvery foliage, so there are *Artemisias* in front. My favourite is A. *alba* **'Canescens'** which has wonderful thread-like curled leaves like silver wire. It is not very well known, but I find it perfectly hardy. It is semi-ever grey but needs cutting back in spring. A little silver shrub for a sunny sheltered spot is *Convolvulus cneorum* with lovely small white flowers. Unlike others of that family, it neither twines nor runs, but makes a neat compact bush. I also have a grey-leafed low growing *Helianthemum*, or **Rock Rose**, with white flowers called *H*. **'The Bride'**, and pink *Diascias*, South African plants which form soft green mats, covered with pink flowers all summer. They are not completely hardy, but root so easily, it is simple to take cuttings to over-winter in a greenhouse or cold frame.

If you have space for a larger shrub, I suggest *Daphne odora 'Aureomarginata'* (syn. *D. odora 'Marginata'*). Like all *Daphnes* it is wonderfully sweet scented and flowers in March and April. If you can plant it near a doorway you will be greeted by a waft of perfume as you open the door. It forms a shapely bush about four feet tall and equally wide. The evergreen leaves have a neat white margin, so it always looks attractive. Another choice would be *Osmanthus delavayi*, also an evergreen bush with small holly-like leaves and clusters of sweetly scented white flowers in May. If all these plants seem rather difficult to find, **Catmint** is a very good choice for the front, which you could combine with the bulbs and perhaps pink *geraniums* or *petunias*.

⚜ PLANTING SHADY BORDERS ⚜

I have tried to give some helpful suggestions for planting schemes in sunny situations, so let us now think about the shady places that we all have in our gardens. There is, of course, a great deal of difference between the plants that like shade because they prefer a damp soil, and those that will tolerate the much more difficult environment of dry shade. If the latter is under deciduous trees, it is not such a problem, as nearly all spring flowering plants, which originate in woodland – and particularly those with bulbs and tubers such as **snowdrops** (*galanthus*), **bluebells** (the large flowered garden variety) *anenomes* and above all *dwarf cyclamen* – will naturalise there, provided that they have light and moisture in winter and spring before the trees come into leaf. The easiest of the little *cyclamen* is the ivy-leafed *C. hederifolium*, which has the added advantage of flowering in autumn, and keeping its lovely marbled leaves, which follow on after the flowers, throughout winter and spring. They die back as the trees come into leaf and the corms then like to keep dry.

However, there are also dry shady places in most gardens under walls or fences or in difficult corners where the problem is not so much lack of light in summer as of dense shade all the year. Here we can think above all in terms of attractive foliage and of trying to improve the soil with humus and mulching. We can then plant *Euphorbias* and *Hellebores* for the spring, *Alchemilla* and *Dicentras* to follow and for a fairly hopeless situation where you need ground cover, try **periwinkles**. *Vinca minor*, the small-leafed variety, is more compact and less invasive, or the dark leafed purple *Ajuga* (Bugle) and **violets**, particularly the dark-leafed variety called *V. labradorica*. Some of the *Lamiums* are also attractive, but beware of the handsome yellow flowered *L. galeobdolon*, which will quickly gallop forward and take over a more favourable situation, smothering other plants as it goes. **Ivies** (*Hedera*) also make dense ground cover, but cannot be trusted to stay where you plant them. **Ferns** are handsome and worthwhile, but not all tolerate dry soil.

Shady places with damp soil are altogether easier to deal with and there is quite a large choice of splendid plants, which prefer not to grow in full sunshine provided that the soil is reasonably moist.

To start with some negatives – **roses** do not enjoy shade. They never seem to grow well without sunshine and air around them. *Clematis* feel the same, but like to have their roots cool and shaded and then to get their heads up into the sun. Nothing that comes from a Mediterranean climate can tolerate much shade; all the grey-leafed plants, many bulbs, *diascias* and *osteospermums* are sun-loving, but of course there are many good-natured plants that will grow in almost any situation if the soil is right.

The real shade lovers include **hydrangeas**, **rhododendrons**, **azaleas** and *sarcococcas* among the shrubs. *Hellebores*, *euphorbias* and, of course, *hostas* will give you handsome foliage. *Fuchsias* will flower throughout late summer and autumn. *Phloxes* too, are happiest without too much sun, as are all the **primroses** (*Primulas*) and **polyanthus** (*primula vulgaris*), which are so lovely in spring.

So for a really shady border I would suggest planning mainly for foliage effect, with *hostas* interplanted with snowdrops and primroses in front, then *Helleborus **orientalis***, with evergreen leaves and purple or greeny-white speckled flowers in April, and *Euphorbia **polychroma***, which dies down in winter but makes a marvellous show of lime green flower heads in spring and early summer. At the back, *hydrangeas*, and particularly a white flowered variety would light up your patch of shade, and if your ground is sufficiently damp, you could try the hardy **Arum lily** (**Zantedeschia aethiopica**). Consider the neat, shiny leaves of *sarcococca*, with small sweetly scented flowers in winter, and the variegated leaves of *Arum **italicum*** subsp. *italicum* 'Marmoratum' (syn. *A. pictum*), which disappear underground in summer. Both would furnish your border in winter, as would the sword-like leaves of ***Iris foetidissima***, a plant that will tolerate the deepest shade.

✣ FLOWERING ON AND ON ✣

AS I write this we enjoy an Indian Summer and autumn colour is everywhere, enhanced by low sunlight – but our gardens can begin to look a bit lack-lustre. I have written about hardy *fuchsias*, of which the most rewarding to me is definitely *F. magellanica* **'Versicolor'**. It is quite a large bush, but as it dies down completely in the winter and will be cut to the ground in early spring, I grow bulbs or early flowering plants around it, and it will take over later to fill in the gaps. Incidentally, the dead branches make excellent plant supports or pea sticks.

I also have several clumps of *Nerines*, the late flowering pink **lily**, revelling in a hot dry position under a wall.

I have added two late-flowering shrubs. The small bright blue grey-leafed *Caryopteris x clandonensis*, is still at its best now, which should be cut right back in spring; and the evergreen *Abelia x grandiflora*, which has hanging clusters of white flowers with rosy-red calyxes. This needs a sheltered position, as it can be cut back by hard frost.

In my mixed border I grow only one **Michaelmas Daisy**, *Aster x frikartii*, which never gets mildew and has large single mauvy-blue flowers lasting until the frosts; and one hardy **chrysanthemum**, a little pom-pom variety. This benefits from careful placing as it needs to be near the front to show well. It can get tall and straggly before flowering, hiding the plants behind it. I find the solution is to cut back the new shoots down to about half when they are growing well in June. They then try again and form a shorter, bushier plant which flowers equally well in autumn. Another late flowerer, still giving of its best, is the prostrate herbaceous *Geranium wallichianum* **'Buxton's Variety'**. It has blue flowers with a white eye, and weaves itself among the surrounding plants. I think this is happiest in semi-shade.

56

❦ SEDUM AUTUMN JOY ❧

CONTINUING my suggestions of plants that flower late, the big *Sedum 'Herbstfreude'* (syn *S.* **Autumn Joy**) is a worthwhile addition to the garden. From the moment the fat blue-green buds first start into growth in late spring until frost finally dims the large cluster heads of tiny purple-pink flowers, it is a pleasure to the eye. When in full flower from late summer onwards, it gives you a large clump of almost bronzy colour, which blends perfectly with autumn foliage. And when it dies, I find the stiff brown flower heads quite useful to weave through small tender shrubs, such as evergreen **azaleas**, to protect their buds from frost damage.

It seems to me to have only one drawback, the plants straggle as they increase in size and the flower heads flop outwards leaving a bare centre. The remedy is to dig them up and split the clumps in late autumn, replanting smaller pieces, but this is quite hard work as the roots are tough. I find the best place to plant them is on a slope, then the flowers will flop downwards in one direction, and you still get a massed colour effect.

Two annuals also help to maintain colour in the autumn garden. Our old friend, **tobacco** *(Nicotiana)*, flowers and flowers. The lime green and white varieties are very popular now, but the pinky purple ones seem just right for autumn. A much newer addition to continuous flowering annuals is the strain of low growing **Busy Lizzies**, *Impatiens walleriana*, which come in such lovely pinks purple, orange and red shades. As they thrive without much sun and can take quite a lot of wet weather, they will go on flowering for months until finally laid low by cold nights.

⚘ TIME TO BUY THE BULBS FOR NEXT SPRING ⚘

BULBS have been in the shops for some time already; but I expect most of us have delayed putting them in while the soil is still hard and dry. It is not too late to plant them in October, but we should certainly think of doing so soon. Some planting tips might be useful.

Unless they are planted deep enough, they run the risk of frost damage and the stems will be weak and flop over. A good general rule for small bulbs is to make the planting hole twice the height of the bulb itself, but never to have more than two inches of soil over the nose of the bulb. **Tulips**, however, like to be much deeper with six inches of soil on top and will live and flower much longer if you do this. Even so, they seem to dwindle over the years. Some time ago, I tried a tip from *Gardener's World* and planted some in deep plastic pots; (some bone-meal in the compost or soil you use is a good idea) and then sank the pots completely in the garden. This is quite successful – they flower well and it is very easy to lift the pots again after they have died back. They generally perform equally well from year to year.

Daffodils (*Narcissus*), too, like to be deep and snug, but they are such tall bulbs that a hole three times their height will install them under four inches of soil. This is not easy when naturalising them in grass, and the alternative method of lifting back the sods in curving lines with a spade works quite well, and gives a very natural effect but do get them in as deep as you can.

Hyacinths (*Hyacinthus*) on the other hand hate being buried too deep. If you grow them in bowls indoors, you should feed them well as the foliage dies back, and then plant them outside in a sunny position in holes twice the depth of the bulb. As they are chunky in shape, they will end up under about two inches of soil and will then increase and flower for years.

Snowdrops (*Galanthus*) hate being dried off and should be planted in spring while the leaves are still green. They prefer a shady situation, and will increase and seed freely if they are happy.

✎ ESTABLISHING BIENNIALS ✎

I have written about a few trouble-free annuals that I grow, and suggested that **forget-me-nots** (*Myosotis*) were a great standby for spring, but, of course, strictly speaking they are not annuals but biennials, as the seedlings for next year are germinating now. **Wallflowers** (*Erysimum ercheiri*), **Sweet Williams** (*Dianthus barbatus*) and **Canterbury Bells** (*Campanula medium*) and many other plants have the same growth cycle, and all flower in the spring or early summer. A true annual such as a **poppy** (*Papaver*) germinates, flowers and dies in the same year.

Other biennials can be established in the garden and will self-seed and form permanent colonies, but do tend to need a little management to see that they all keep their place and flower to advantage. **Foxgloves** (*Digitalis*) are a good example. They are so prolific that it is wise to pull up the dead flower spikes before they seed, or they will be all over the garden. It is also easy to find yourself with a fine display every alternate year. Such handsome flowers, but I wish they did not end up with a ridiculous little tuft of purple or white at the top of a tall spike of green seed pods.

If you can find room for them the biennial **thistles** are

handsome plants. The tall silver **Onopordum** is a spectacular sight, up to six feet in height. Once you have grown one, you will find the odd seedling appearing for years to come.

More useful is the biennial *Eryngium giganteum*, **Miss Willmott's ghost**, with blue-green leaves and a pale blue centred flower surrounded by a pale grey ruff. They glimmer in the evening light, and Miss Willmott must have loved them as they were given her name. They do seed freely, but do not spread it with such abandon, so it is fairly simple to keep them in a group.

Another exciting large biennial is the tall ***Salvia turkestanica***, with woolly leaves and an unforgettable mauve-pink flower spike. I was given a seedling a few years ago, which flowered that summer and died, and two years later two of its seedlings flowered. They are wonderful in the Hatfield garden, where I am always being asked what they are.

❧ VARIEGATED LEAVES ☙

COLOUR variation in leaves takes many different and attractive forms. It became popular in the last century when many new non-hardy plants were introduced to be grown in Victorian greenhouses and conservatories, and variegated hollies and spotted laurels were planted in shrubberies – along whose winding paths ladies could take exercise without trailing their skirts in damp grass. There were always gardeners to tend the potted plants and garden boys to keep the paths weed free.

Two great gardeners, Gertrude Jekyll and William Robertson inspired the planting of flower borders for colour and effect, but their plantings relied largely on herbaceous and bedding plants. Now we aim to make our gardens both labour saving and attractive all the year round, and we are much more interested in mixed borders of shrubs and perennials where the colour and texture of leaves is as important as the succession of flowers.

When it comes to choosing variegated plants, we all have our favourites, but I doubt if many of us would want spotted **laurels** (*Laurus nobilis*). If you ask yourself why you prefer laurels with plain green leaves, the answer might be that spots on leaves are sometimes a sign of disease, as in black spot on roses. In fact all variegation is a form of virus, so it is worth remembering that no variegated plant will grow as vigorously as its green counterpart. This can, of course, be a great advantage. A variegated **holly** (*Ilex*) will never make as tall a tree as a green one, and a variegated **ivy** (*Hedera*) or **periwinkle** (*Vinca*) will never take over the whole garden. *Ajuga* or Bugle is another example. The variegated forms are attractive and well behaved, and the green one is a thug. Fortunately there is no green *lamium* that I know of as the variegated ones are quite aggressive enough.

On the whole, I prefer green and white variegation to green and yellow, with few exceptions such as the glossy gold-splashed leaves of *Elaeagnus 'Maculata'*. I find the variegated *Euonymus* a most useful plant which will either make a rounded bush or clothe the base of a wall without flopping forward, but would choose the E. fortunei **'Emerald Gaiety'** or *E. f.* **'Silver Queen'** rather than *E. f.* **'Emerald and Gold'**. Among herbaceous plants I like the variegated *Astrantia major* which has very handsome green and white leaves, the stripey grasses, ivy-leafed **geranium** and the beautiful white-flowered *Lunaria annua 'Alba variegata'* or **Honesty** whose leaves are liberally splashed with white.

✎ HYDRANGEAS ✌

MUCH of the interest and colour of our September gardens is provided by a very well known family of plants, the *Hydrangeas*. First the **Mop-heads**, or *H. macrophyllas 'Hortensias'*, to give them their correct name. In France, all hydrangeas are known as *hortensias*, and there is a delightful story of an elderly French botanist in the 18th century who went on a round-the-world plant collecting expedition by sailing ship, and took his mistress along disguised as a young male assistant. No one discovered the secret of her sex until they arrived at Tahiti, when a local chief asked for her hand in marriage. Her name, of course, was Hortense. The mop-heads were collected in Mauritius.

Their most interesting characteristic – unique as far as I know – is the way in which they change colour according to the amount of lime in the soil. If your soil is acid, you can enjoy the brilliant blue varieties, but in an alkaline soil, the same plant will turn bright sugar pink. The white ones, my favourites, will remain white everywhere until they become tinged with rusty pink as they age, and the deep pink ones simply take on a deeper purple shade in really acid soil.

My soil is about neutral, and interestingly enough, the first *hydrangeas* I planted were a good blue. Then gradually they changed to produce some blue flowers still, but also some mauve ones. Even more curious, all cuttings from these plants start sugar pink, and then gradually change back again with a few more mauve and blue flowers each year. The effect of all these colours on one plant is rather fascinating; I believe that this change is probably caused by top dressings of acid leaf mould, yet the cuttings were struck in a lime-free peat compost.

The great charm of the *hydrangea* lies in the fact that they age rather than wither as the flowers die. The petals become papery and glow with rich colour, the blue ones turning metallic green and the pinks marvellous purples and rich reds. This is the moment to pick them for drying, and I find the most satisfactory method is to arrange them in water in a warm room and just do not bother to top up the water. As it dries up, so will the *hydrangea* heads.

At the first real frost the flowers still on the plant turn brown. It is wise not to cut them off until spring, as they will protect next year's buds against frost and cold wind. Then cut them off and tidy up and feed the plants – never in the autumn as late pruning or feeding will encourage fresh growth, which might be frost-damaged.

I was recently asked why *hydrangeas* fail to flower, which is not a problem in this garden. The best advice I can find is to feed them well and make sure they are never short of water. Although they grow well in the shade, very few plants will flower well unless they get some sun during the day, which may be the cause of the problem.

⚘ GRASSES ⚘

IN the last few years the idea of growing ornamental grasses in our gardens has become very popular. They are not always easy to place as they look best on their own, uncrowded by other plants, so that their leaves and feathery seed heads can wave in the wind, adding textures and interest to the garden in autumn and winter. By the spring they begin to look tatty and it is best to cut them down which will encourage new growth.

They associate very well with low-growing plants, which flower early in the summer such as herbaceous **geraniums** or **alchemilla**. These can be trimmed back after flowering and will form a carpet of fresh leaves but are unlikely to produce many more flowers. The taller grasses will rise above them and show to advantage.

There are many different families, most of which have impossible names. Some are happiest in damp soil, others like it sunny and well drained, but the majority are not fussy and will grow well in any reasonable soil. They often have handsome variegated leaves but it is wise to avoid the invasive ones such as the well-known **"Gardener's Garters"** (*Phalaris arundinacea*).

I find the *stipas* the most effective, *S. arundinacea* is really beautiful, with arching clumps of foliage which develop autumn colouring of rich golden orange, *S. gigantea* is even taller, four to five feet high with superb flower heads. It makes a splendid feature at the back of the border, beautiful all summer. My very favourite is *S. tenuissima*; much shorter, for the front, with fine hair-like foliage and delicate silky flower heads that move in the slightest breeze. The *Carex* or **sedges** are also eye catching. They prefer a damp soil by the water's edge or in shade among trees.

Finally, two much shorter ones. The *Festucas* have stiff needle-like foliage and will grow in hot dry positions in full sun. They make vivid tufts of blue or yellow green. *Milium effusum 'Aureum'* or **Bowles' golden grass** makes clumps of soft foliage, bright yellow in spring, which will grow in shade and light up a dark corner.

⚜ AUTUMN COLOUR ⚜

I began to think about the whole question of autumn colour recently when a friend who knows this garden well, surprised me by saying it looked at its best in October because it was so colourful then.

The main effect comes, of course, from the glowing colour of turning leaves, chrome yellow and russet red, enhanced by the highlights of late flowers; a few **roses** perhaps, an abundance of *fuchsias*, the bronze heads of *Sedum* **Autumn Joy**, an occasional patch of mauve or violet **Michaelmas daisies** (*Aster*) and the vital highlights of silvery grey foliage. Of course, it all looks rather better from a distance when the gaps left by dead or dying plants are less noticeable!

So the first consideration is to mass the plants which give this effect at some distance from the house, and preferably beyond the cool green stretch of lawn – and then take trouble to cut down and tidy up any other plants as they die down.

We are fortunate to be able to grow **azaleas** and to have **beech** trees as a background, all of which colour early while the weather is still pleasant. *Parrotia persica* is a small spreading tree, which turns a wonderful pinky red, and there are also *Acers* (Maples) and *Cornuses*. Our native maple is the *sycamore* (*Acer pseudoplatanus*), which is rather a disaster in a garden, as its leaves frequently develop black blotches and drop early, looking very unsightly. In addition, it seeds prolifically and in fact, is one of my pet hates. It is the **Japanese maples** (*Acer palmatum*) which are so desirable. *A. p.* *'Osakazuki'* is probably the most colourful, turning fiery scarlet in the autumn, and would look wonderful against a dark green background.

Curiously enough, the **Canadian maples**, which give such a marvellous show each "fall", are not hardy in England. They survive the harsh Canadian winters, but here would break into growth in every mild spell and then suffer frost damage.

Pyracanthas are very effective shrubs on walls and are quite happy with a north aspect. Their brilliant red berries made a

splendid show in winter until the birds devour them in a cold
spell.

◁ HARDY FERNS ▷

I wonder if any of my readers have already found a shady
corner in which to grow hardy ferns. The Victorians loved
them, and Miss Jekyll planted them extensively in her woodland
garden, about which she wrote so entrancingly. Now that
gardeners are once more appreciating what fascinating plants
they are, it is possible to find them at good plant nurseries, and
some specialists sell quite a wide range of varieties.

My "fernery" is quite tiny, about two and a half feet by two feet
in the shade of a north facing wall, so I only have room for
three contrasting varieties.   The first one, which I was given as
a small plant, and which inspired me to find others, is the most
spectacular. All ferns have impossibly long Latin names, but
fortunately most of them have acquired a more manageable
English one, and this is known as the **Mother and Child** fern
(*Asplenium bulbiferum*). It has the great merit of being
evergreen with very handsome large leaves developing from the
'Bishop's Crozier' buds, which slowly unfurl their fresh green
fronds each spring. At the same time last season's dark leaves
are developing a bright green rib of tiny seedling leaves, which
slowly grow into little plantlets, which can be detached from
mother and grown on to make new plants.

As this has become quite a large fern, it takes up most of my
available space, but beside it I have placed a **Hart's Tongue**
(*Asplenium scolopendrium*) whose narrow upright leaves make
a good contrast, and in front a feathery little lady fern, called, I
believe, the **Oak Fern** (*Gymnocarpium dryopteris*), which dies
away in winter.

Most of us already have the common male fern, which turns up uninvited in damp shady places. It always looks quite handsome, but does die down in winter. The majority of ferns are categorised as either "male" or "lady". This has nothing to do with their sex, but refers to their habit of growth, the boys having stiff leaves with a central rib, and the girls a soft feathery one.

❧ NERINES ❧

AS I write this, the most striking feature in the garden is a narrow border under our south windows where the *Nerines* are coming into flower. They will still be there well into November when the first frosts may well have browned the **hydrangeas** and blackened all the **dahlias** and **fuchsias**.

One of the most attractive members of the **lily** family, *Nerines* come from South Africa and revel in a well-drained situation, such as the base of a south or west-facing wall. Like so many plants from hot, dry climates, they have large bulbs for storing the goodness manufactured by copious sword-like leaves. These come up in early spring and start dying back before the tall stems crowned with clusters of bright pink flowers with back curling petals, finally thrust up in the autumn.

Exquisite as these flowers are, their bare stems are rather ungainly on their own and look infinitely better if you plant something silvery grey in front of them. The invaluable *Helichrysum petiolare* (syn. *petiolatum*), which will weave its long sprays covered with round felty silver leaves over quite a large area, sets off the pink *nerine* flowers perfectly. It seldom lives through the winter, but is easily propagated by cuttings taken in autumn and wintered in a greenhouse or sheltered frame. Any of the low growing *Artemisias* would look good too.

Nerines are not rich feeders and seem to thrive best in poor, dry soil and positively slum conditions. The bulbs increase at a tremendous rate until it seems as if they were pushing each other out of the soil.

I used to think that these bulbs were quite frost resistant and could be safely moved at any time in the winter when they were dormant, as I have often done in the past. Years ago, I decided that mine all needed dividing and replanting. Fortunately, this proved such a daunting task, that I only tackled one large clump. All those I replanted died in the prolonged frost of that February.

I can now only suggest that if you buy or are given bulbs in the winter, they should be covered and protected until the danger of hard frost is over.

⚜ HARDY FUCHSIAS ⚜

HARDY *fuchsias* are a great standby in the October garden. Fortunately, we have had few really early frosts in the past few years, and they have continued to flower into November.

Later on, a little protection, such as a collar of dried bracken, is probably a help to those that might not survive a really hard winter, but I have never lost one completely. It is a mistake to cut them back until spring, when you can see the shoots beginning to develop at the base of the bare branches. Of course, any grown as standards will need to be dug up and potted, to spend the winter in shelter, as they never break in the open except at ground level. It is wiser in any case to keep standards permanently in pots or tubs, which you can move into the greenhouse together with the non-hardy varieties before the first frosts.

The protected ones will flower much earlier, from May onwards, whereas left in the open ground they do not come into flower until July. Keep them almost dry all the winter and prune and shape them in January or early February when they are at their most dormant. At any other time the sap will be rising and they will drip from every cut and will exhaust the plant. As the cuts seal up, it is safe to start re-potting, watering and feeding. I find it beneficial to knock them all out of their pots – remove some of the old compost and replace it with fresh. Keep a sharp look-out for the white grubs of vine weevils as you do this – they love *fuchsias* and might be found at the bottom of their pots, feeding on the roots.

Those left in the open ground can be cut down and given some general fertiliser from March onwards.

Best value to me in the autumn garden is *F. magellanica var. gracilis* **'Tricolor'** grown for its delightful foliage, variegated in deep rose-pink red and cream. The flowers are deep red, small and neat, as in all the *magellanica Fuchsias*, and it is completely hardy, making a larger bush every year with graceful arching branches up to four feet in height.

I do not know the names of all my other hardy fuchsias, as I struck them from cuttings given to me by my friends, but reliable ones to try are *F.* **'Lena'**, large flowered with a pink trumpet and purple falls, *F.* **'Mrs. Popple'**, with purple and red flowers, and *F.* **'Dollar Princess'**, a dwarfer variety only about 15 inches high and particularly attractive, with a frilled red double trumpet and purple falls.

All fuchsias root so easily from cuttings taken at any time during the summer that it is worthwhile to experiment with leaving any of them in the ground provided you have some young replacement plants in your greenhouse. Many varieties said to be non-hardly are really semi-hardy and will survive happily in a mild winter.

✖ PUTTING THE GARDEN TO BED ✖

IT is difficult in a mild autumn to get started on putting the garden to bed, but another severe winter is always on the cards, so it is as well to take precautions.

Plants in containers are the most vulnerable. If the soil in a pot freezes it will take a very long time to thaw out again, and an earthenware container may well crack. To wrap it in bubble plastic or a polythene sack stuffed with straw or dead leaves would prevent this happening.

Plants and shrubs that are newly planted are particularly at risk, and a good mulch over their roots would be a wise precaution. Evergreens need water all the time and can die of drought in a prolonged frost. A mulch will help to prevent this. Bracken fronds are one of the most useful materials. I always use them to cover up *nerine* and *agapanthus* bulbs and the roots of *fuchsias*. You can also lace them into the top of small evergreens such as dwarf *rhododendrons* to protect the buds.

If we do get heavy snow, do not forget to go round knocking it off evergreens before it freezes on the leaves and the weight breaks the branches.

Grey plants and small alpines dislike rain more than cold. Always try to give them sharp drainage.

Small plants can be kept dry under a pane of glass or a cloche, but make sure there is plenty of air circulation or they may rot just the same.

❧ WHICH TREE TO PLANT ❧

ONE of the most important choices in a garden must always be which tree to plant, and, of course, this depends on area and aspect. If you had a really big lawn you could plant something exotic like a **Tulip tree** (*Liriodendron tulipifera*) or a ***Catalpa*** that have lovely leaves and flowers and a good shape, but are too large for the average garden. For a smaller area I would suggest a **Mulberry** (*Morus nigra*) or a **Quince** (*Cydonia*). Quinces are particularly attractive with pale silvery-green leaves, white flowers and beautiful golden fruit in the autumn. If it is a reasonably sheltered position and you want flowers, nothing is lovelier than a ***Magnolia stellata*** for the small garden and *M x **soulangeana*** if you have more space.

I suppose the **Cherry** tree is the best known and loved of all flowering trees and I think the most beautiful is *Prunus 'Taihaku'* – the **Great White Cherry** from Japan, whose double white flowers open out among the bronze leaf buds. The leaves turn green later, but colour well in the autumn. Another good choice would be a standard **Maytree**. *Crataegus persimilis 'Prunifolia'* is probably the best form with pink or white flowers in May and wonderful autumn colour. It is also completely hardy and will grow in any soil. An ***Amelanchier*** is another charming small tree – very pretty in spring with white flowers and good autumn colour – but does lose its leaves rather early in autumn. As does ***Parrotia persica***, always the first to colour for me, but unequalled in glowing purpley red. And, of course, the popular ***Robinia pseudoacacia 'Frisia'*** is a beautiful yellow all summer, but does I think look better among other trees and preferably against a dark background.

Finally, do not forget that many of our native trees enjoy colonising gardens uninvited, and keep a sharp look out for invading seedlings. **Sycamore** (*Acer pseudoplatanus*) and **Ash** (*Fraxinus*) are the most persistent. If you find them young enough they are easy to pull up, but after two or three years it is quite a different story and they love to get their roots under walls or tangled up among your favourite shrubs.

✦ SHRUBS WORTH GROWING ✦

WHEN I was writing about some of my favourite trees, I began to wonder which shrubs I find most rewarding in the garden.

I am fortunate to have neutral to acid soil, but I know many gardeners in this area cannot grow lime-hating plants like **rhododendrons** and **azaleas**, so I will leave them out. There are many shrubs I would miss more.

Starting with some evergreens, ***Osmanthus delavayi*** is a small shrub with neat shiny leaves, flowering in May with a profusion of sweet-scented white flowers. If unpruned it will grow to four or five feet, but you can trim it after flowering and keep it to any size you want. Before that in early spring the clusters of small tubular pink flowers on ***Daphne odora 'Aureomarginata'*** (syn. *Daphne odora 'Marginata'*) fill my whole courtyard with their delicious scent. This *daphne* is a low sprawling bush and the leaves have narrow white margins. I could not bear to prune it except when it blocks the door out of the house. All it needs is a sunny sheltered corner and good drainage.

May is also the month for the lovely blue ***Ceanothus*** of which there are so many good varieties. Again they are not fully hardy and need the protection of a wall. The low growing ground covering variety *C. **thyrsiflorus** var. repens* has survived many winters with me and is one of my favourites.

Scent is so important that everyone should plant a ***Philadelphus***, nothing else smells so intoxicatingly sweet in

June. There are many varieties and all are hardy and undemanding, so which one you choose depends on how much space you can give it. *P.* **'Belle Etoile'** is one of the best and is medium sized – five or six feet tall.

Among the smaller shrubs ***Potentillas*** are invaluable as they flower continuously all summer. My favourite is the white *P. fruticosa* **'Manchu'**. The hardiest and most eye-catching of the silver-leafed shrubs is ***Senecio greyi***. Bright yellow flowers cover the whole bush in June and July and you should cut it back after flowering or else prune it hard in April, which will stop it flowering and keep it in shape.

Later in the summer ***hydrangeas*** give us welcome colour and I particularly enjoy the tall lace-cap ***H. villosa***. You should have a ***buddleia*** for scent and butterflies and here my choice is the grey-leafed *B.* **'Lochinch'**. Another invaluable autumn shrub is the pink and grey foliaged ***Fuchsia magellanica* 'Versicolor'**. Like all the hardy *fuchsias* it dies right down in winter and you cut it to the ground in early spring. Another attractive late-flowering shrub is ***Abelia x grandiflora***, at its best in September. This has pretty soft green foliage and white flowers with pink calyx. It is semi-evergreen and may lose its leaves in a hard winter.

❦ WINTER FLOWERING SHRUBS ❧

IT is a rather surprising fact that almost all winter flowering shrubs are very sweetly scented. It seems unlikely that there are many insect pollinators about in January and February to be attracted by such delicious smells, but these shrubs come mainly from the Far East, where perhaps their attendant moths and bees have a different life style. If you bring their twigs covered with fragile little flowers in from the cold winter garden, they will scent a room for days.

It is not always easy to know where best to place these shrubs in the garden as they do need a sheltered position, yet do not contribute much interest in the summer. The most fragrant of all, the **'Wintersweet'** (*Chimonanthus*), does have lovely leaves, long and pointed, growing in bunches like the fingers of a hand in a rather elegant Chinese way. I think it can look very attractive at the back of a wide border with the protection of a wall, where it will grow up to 10 feet tall. It is very slow to flower and you may have to wait up to seven years before its bare winter twigs are covered with little yellow flowers with a dark centre and a quite amazing perfume.

Hamamelis mollis, the **Chinese Witch-hazel**, is a rather less distinguished looking shrub with leaves closely resembling our native **hazel**. The bare twigs are also covered with little yellow flowers, but these have curious thin twisted petals resembling a burst of tiny fire crackers and again, are very sweetly scented. *Hamamelis x intermedia* **'Pallida'** is considered the best form with rather paler flowers than *H. mollis*. They are always expensive shrubs to buy, being both difficult to propagate and slow growing, but they do flower freely when still quite young.

I can no longer find room for another shrub from China, the winter flowering **honeysuckle,** *Lonicera x purpusii*. The tiny white flowers smell quite intoxicating but like all honeysuckles, it is a rampant grower. It does not climb but makes a large bush and needs a sunny position to flower well. Perhaps one should overcome its summer drabness by growing a *clematis* through it.

The winter flowering *Viburnums* also make large bushes with still upright growth and clusters of white or pink flowers. Again for the back of the border, but they do need a sunny position to flower well. I prefer the white form, *V. farreri* but the pink hybrid, *V. x bodnantense*, is the hardiest and flowers most freely. They can be damaged by frost but in mild winters are a glorious sight and again smell intensely sweet.

Finally, the invaluable evergreens; ***Mahonia japonica*** has beautiful long pinnate leaves carried in whorls at about 12 inch intervals on stiff upright stems. The topmost bunch produces a fat flower bud, which opens into long hanging racemes of pale yellow bells, which resemble and have a similar scent to **lily of the valley** (*convallaria*). It will tolerate some shade and is a spectacular shrub to fill an angle between two walls. In complete contrast, the humble little ***Sarcococca*** is a neat little evergreen of the **box** (*buxus*) family, only about a foot high, with glossy green leaves. It will flourish in any awkward shady corner and its tiny white flowers open in February and smell deliciously sweet.

⚔ FAVOURITE TOOLS ⚓

WHAT shall we give our gardening friends for Christmas?

All the Bos products are invaluable. The Bos sheet of strong plastic has handles at the four corners and you can throw prunings etc. on it before gathering them up for the bonfire, or transport a plant you are moving without spilling soil from its roots.

The useful Bos bag opens up to sit firmly on the ground while you throw in your weeds or autumn leaves before transporting to the compost heap. The Bos apron is far from elegant, but made from a strong waterproof plastic with a large and deep enough pocket for keeping secateurs, labels, etc. without fear of them falling out as you bend over your plants.

Careless gardeners like me should have all our smaller tools with red handles to ensure they do not get mislaid and end up on a bonfire or compost heap. I always wish someone would produce red gardening gloves to save them from the same fate. Red-handled Felco secateurs are quite simply the best as well as the most expensive you can buy, but should last a lifetime. I have two other red-handled treasures made by Wolf Tools; a six inch flat steel pike about an inch wide which I use for weeding and prefer to a hand fork, and one-handled shears which adjust to use sideways or flat. These are excellent for trimming back plants after flowering as you have a hand free to collect the trimmings. I also use them for edging the lawn.

Wolf also make a small short-handled hoe, rather like an old fashioned onion hoe, which I also find very useful.

∂ GARDENING BOOKS ∕∘

ALL the great gardeners who have influenced the development of gardens over the years have one thing in common: they wrote books in which we can still study their ideas.

There are now so many books available on all aspects of gardening that the choice is almost bewildering. Perhaps a brief account of those I have found most helpful might be of use. First and foremost is a *Dictionary of Garden Plants* from the RHS or *The Reader's Digest*. I have the original RHS one, not so complete, but I think easier to use than the latest one. On the whole I think *The Reader's Digest* is perhaps the best.

For basic principles of design read Russell Page's *The Education of a Gardener*. Two other old favourites of mine are Christopher Lloyd's *The Well-Tempered Garden* and Robin Lane Fox's *Better Gardening*. Beth Chatto's *The Dry Garden* and *The Wet Garden* are helpful and informative, and her *Garden*

Diary is a delight. All of these should still be available in paperback.

A really lovely book that came out recently is *Penelope Hobhouse on Gardening* – her description of the famous National Trust Garden at Tintenhall in Somerset, where she lived and worked for many years, and of the plants grown there. She gives practical chapters on all her excellent methods of cultivation, taking cuttings, sowing seeds etc., which are excellent and the illustrations are superb – although I do not personally find glossy photographs of wonderful plant combinations are much help when it comes to planting your own borders.

❧ THE MUSEUM OF GARDEN HISTORY ❧

MANY gardeners and plant lovers will by now have heard of, and perhaps visited, the Museum of Garden History.

It is housed in the historic church of St. Mary's, Lambeth, where the John Tradescants, father and son, are buried. This church was redundant and derelict in 1977, when the Tradescant Trust was set up to save the building from demolition, and turn it into the world's first Museum of Garden History and a centre for lectures and exhibitions relating to gardening. The fabric is now fully restored; the Museum is small, but fascinating, and part of the Churchyard has become a seventeenth century garden designed by Lady Salisbury and planted with contemporary plants.

This peaceful little churchyard contains the tomb of the two Tradescants, gardeners to the first Lord Salisbury at Hatfield, to the Duke of Buckingham, to King Charles I and to Queen Henrietta Maria. They could also be described as the first of a long line of British plant collectors, and they brought back from their travels in Europe and America many of the flowers, shrubs and trees that we still enjoy today. Another famous tomb is that of Captain Bligh of the "Bounty", now considered a much-maligned character. His ill-fated voyage was an attempt to collect seedlings of the **breadfruit tree** from Tahiti, to be established in the West Indies in an attempt to improve the diet of plantation slaves. Joseph Banks, the famous botanist who sailed with Captain Cook, and was one of the founders of Kew Gardens, sponsored it.

In 1993 an appeal was launched by the Trust to finance the expansion of the Museum by making galleries at first floor level to house the exhibits. This was divided into six sections from medieval times to the present day, showing paintings, maps, engravings and photographs, with tools and garden furniture, models and a continuing plant theme. This left the ground floor free for temporary exhibitions and lectures, etc. A garden information centre and reference library was established, and the restaurant facilities enlarged and improved.

❧ LIST OF PLANT NAMES ❧

All plant names have been checked for spelling and accuracy against the following sources:
RHS Plant Finder 2002
RHS A-Z Encyclopaedia of Garden Plants, 1998
Elsevier's Dictionary of Plant Names and their origin, D.C. Watts 2000

AGM refers to Award of Garden Merit.

All page references are against the Latin names of plants, with cross-references from any English names also included in the text.